EP Math 4

Parent's Guide

Welcome to the EP Math 4 Parent's Guide!

This little book was created to help you go offline while following EP's Math 4 curriculum. You will need the Math 4 student workbook for your child. Without the online lessons, you will need to be your child's teacher. The directions are here for introducing new topics. The workbook will provide practice and review.

This book also includes objectives for each lesson, materials marked where needed, directions for what to do each lesson, and the complete answer key.

This year includes mental math and this book has the questions to read out loud to your child. They have no problems written in their books, just places for the answers. They are to just compute in their heads and write the answer down. This year they are introduced to long division and working with percent. There are step-by-step directions for working through problems.

Each lesson has a worksheet listed. If you haven't gotten to that part of the lesson yet but have reached the bottom of the page, look to the next page to keep going.

And a little note: To avoid calling all children "he" or the awkward phrasing of "him or her," I've used the plural pronoun when referring to your child, such as, "Take a look at the example problem on their worksheet."

Have a great year.

Lee

Review

Lesson 1

- Students will: read analog clocks, round numbers to the nearest ten and hundred
- Lesson 1 worksheet
  - Take a look at it together to determine if your child needs any review. Here are the key points to make sure they know.
    - Part A: Make sure they know the hour and minute hand and can count by fives around the numbers on the clock to find the minutes. Also, they need to know the current hour is the number that was last passed.
    - Part B: You can look at the first one as an example. 52 is between 50 and 60, so one of those is the answer. Is 52 closer to 50 or 60? (50) When a number ends in five, we round it up.
    - Part C: Rounding to the nearest hundred. Is 192 closer to 100 or 200? If a number ends in 50, we round up. 150 would round to 200.

Lesson 2

- Students will: identify time phrases, add the value of a collection of coins, write numbers into the thousands, round thousands to the nearest hundred
- Lesson 2 worksheet
  - Use the worksheet to make sure your child remembers what to do.
    - Part A: The key words are quarter and half. If your child isn't sure what those are, have them find halfway around the clock on the Lesson 1 page of the workbook, 30 minutes. They can divide the clock in quarters and see that each quarter is fifteen minutes.
      - Half past one is 30 minutes past one o'clock.
      - Quarter past is 15 minutes past the hour.
      - Quarter to is 15 minutes to go to get to the next hour, in other words, 45 minutes.
    - Part B: Ask your child the value of dimes (10 cents), quarters (25 cents), nickels (5 cents), and pennies (1 cent).
    - Part C: They just have to write the numbers.
    - Part D: They are rounding to the nearest hundred. The thousands will stay the same unless it's something with 900 that will round up to the next thousand. Here's an example: 1358 – They just need to look at the 358. Is it closer to 300 or 400? 400 So 1358 rounds to 1400.

1

Lesson3

- Students will: tell time to the minute, identify 3D shapes, read a bar graph
- Lesson 3 worksheet
  - I think they should be able to tackle this on their own.
    - Part A: Each line on the clock is one minute.
    - Part B: They should do what they are sure of first and then see what's left.
    - Part C: There is a key that shows what each line on the graph means.

Lesson 4

- Students will: draw the time, add with regrouping
- Lesson 4 worksheet
  - Part A: They can turn back to a previous page if they need to see a clock for help.
  - Part B: There is an example on the page: $59 + 83$.
    - Nine plus three equals twelve. They write the two in the ones column and the one in the tens column.

tens	ones	
1		
5	9	
8	3	
14	2	=> 142

Lesson 5

- Students will: translate visual representations of fractions into written fractions, subtract double digits with regrouping
- Lesson 5 worksheet
  - Part A: The denominator, the bottom number, is the total number of pieces. The numerator, the top number, is the number of shaded pieces.
  - Part B: There is an example on the page: $74 - 58$.
    - You can't take eight away from four, so you take one group of ten away from the tens' column. We add that ten to the four to get 14. Now we can subtract 14 minus 8.

tens	ones	
6	14	
7̶	4	
5	8	
1	6	=> 16

Lesson 6

- Students will: multiply, add and subtract money with decimals
- Lesson 6+ worksheet
  - They are to do the first section on the page. They should know their facts. If they don't, please work on them using Xtra Math and games online or flashcards and math facts books offline. Math will be easier, and therefore more fun, when they know the answers!
- Lesson 6 worksheet
  - They just need to make sure they are carrying the decimal point into the answer, straight down. With money there are always two digits after the decimal point. They also should remember to label their answer with the money symbol.
  - One last note: there is addition and subtraction. Does your child need to be warned to pay attention to which one they should be doing?

Lesson 7

- Students will: practice division facts, add three-digit numbers, find estimated sums when rounding to the nearest hundred
- Lesson 6+ worksheet
  - These are division facts today. Again, make sure your child is working on mastering facts. That means not only finding the answers, but having them at the tip of their fingers.
- Lesson 7 worksheet
  - They are to find the exact answer to the first four. They will need to "carry" and regroup to find the answers.
  - All of them they should round to the nearest hundred.
    - Anything ending in 50 rounds up.
    - 950 is between nine hundred and ten hundred, namely one thousand. 950 would round to 1000.

Lesson 8

- Students will: practice multiplication facts, subtract three-digit numbers, find estimated differences when rounding to the nearest hundred
- Lesson 6+ worksheet
  - They need to do the next section.
- Lesson 8 worksheet
  - They are to find the exact answer to the first four. They will need to "borrow" and regroup to find the answers.
  - All of them they should round to the nearest hundred.

Lesson 9

- Students will: practice division facts, find sums of four digit numbers, estimate sums by rounding to the nearest hundred and thousand
- Lesson 6+ worksheet (next section)
- They have numbers in the thousands today.
    - To round to the nearest hundred they will look at the tens just like they've been doing. The thousands stay the same unless the hundred is a 9 that's going to round up to 10.
    - To round to the nearest thousand they need to look at the digit before it, the hundred. If it's five hundred and up, then the number rounds up to the next thousand. Here are a few to try.
        - 1299 What thousands is it between?
            - 1000 and 2000 Which is it closer to?
                - 1000 (200 is less than 500, so it rounds down.)
        - 5820
            - It's between 5000 and 6000 and it's closer to 6000.
            - 800 is 500 or more, so it rounds up.
        - 7500
            - It's between 7000 and 8000.
            - When it's in the middle, 500, we round up.
- Lesson 9 worksheet
    - You might want to point out part C! They don't have to find the exact answer to all of them, but you could offer a reward for finding the exact answer to all of them.

Lesson 10

- Students will: round to the nearest ten and hundred, find the difference between four digit numbers, estimate differences by rounding to the nearest hundred and thousand
- Lesson 6+ worksheet
    - They will need to round to the nearest ten and hundred.
        - What is 836 to the nearest ten?
            - They will look at the digit to the right, the ones. 6 is more than 5, so it rounds up. 30 will become 40. The answer is 840.
        - What is 3024 to the nearest ten?
            - Four is less than five, so it rounds down: 24 becomes 20. The answer is 3020.
- Lesson 10 worksheet
    - This is just like Lesson 9's worksheet. They need to pay attention to what they should be rounding to. They only need to find the exact answer to four of them. You could offer a reward for doing them all.

Place Value and Expanded Notation

Lesson 11

- Students will: multiply, write numbers in standard and expanded form
- Expanded form takes a number and breaks it apart by place value.
  - 2547 is 2 thousands and 5 hundreds and 4 tens and 7 ones
  - In expanded form we write it simply: 2000 + 500 + 40 + 7.

Thousands	Hundreds	Tens	Ones
2	5	4	7
1	8	0	0

- You can read the numbers write off the place value chart. We just did 2547. The next number is 1800, one thousand eight hundred. How would it be written in expanded form?
  - 1000 + 800   There's no need to write the zeros. Adding on zeros doesn't change the value at all.
- Lesson 11+ worksheet
  - They will do the first section, multiplication problems. They should do them as fast as they can.
- Lesson 11 worksheet
  - They will write numbers either in standard form, just a regular number, or in expanded form, broken into place value and added together.

Lesson 12

- Students will: divide, write numbers in expanded and standard form
- Lesson 11 + worksheet
  - They should do the next section and divide.
- Lesson 12 worksheet
  - Look at this together. They are going to write their expanded numbers vertically. Each column shows a place value. Then they will add the ones, tens, hundreds, etc. and their answer will be in standard form.

Lesson 13

- Students will: multiply, write numbers in standard and expanded form
- Lesson 11 + worksheet
  - They should do the next section, multiplication.
- Lesson 13 worksheet
  - They should be able to do this, writing numbers in expanded and standard form.

Lesson 14 (scissors)

- Students will: practice division facts, read numbers into the millions
- Practice reading some numbers together.
    - 1 one
    - 21 twenty-one
    - 321 three hundred twenty-one
    - 4,321 four thousand, three hundred twenty-one
        - After each comma you read the following pattern: hundreds, tens, ones. At the comma you say thousand, million, billion, etc.
    - 54,321 fifty-four thousand, three hundred twenty-one
    - 654,321 six hundred fifty-four thousand, three hundred twenty-one
    - 7,654,321 seven million, six hundred fifty-four thousand, three…
    - 87,654,321 eighty-seven million, six hundred fifty-four thousand,…
    - 987,654,321 nine hundred eight-seven million, six hundred…
    - 1,000,000,000 one billion
    - 1,000,000,000,000 one trillion
    - Just for fun…how would you read 6,723,572,894,136?
        - six trillion, seven hundred twenty-three billion, five hundred seventy-two million, eight hundred ninety-four thousand, one hundred thirty-six
- Lesson 11+ worksheet
    - They need to do the next section, which is division facts.
- Lesson 14 worksheet
    - They are to combine the numbers to make bigger numbers and then read them to you.
    - Then they are to write any seven of the big numbers they make in the first column of the Lesson 15 worksheet.

Lesson 15

- Students will: practice addition facts, write numbers in expanded form and in word form into the millions
- Lesson 11+ worksheet
    - They have addition facts today to keep them fresh.

- Lesson 15 worksheet
  - They should already have big numbers written in the first column of the page. That was supposed to be done on Lesson 14.
  - They are to write them in expanded form and then in words.
    - There's a separate page with number words to help them with spelling. Make sure your child knows the form (eg. twenty-eight).

Lesson 16

- Students will: practice multiplication facts, practice place value to the hundred millions
- Read these numbers together.
  - 254   2 hundreds   5 tens   4 ones
    - two hundred fifty-four
  - 863,000   8 hundreds   6 tens   3 ones
    - eight hundred sixty-three thousand
    - When you get to the comma, you say thousand.
  - 792,000,000   7 hundreds   9 tens   2 ones
    - seven hundred ninety-two million
    - When you get to the comma, you say million.
  - 792,863,254
    - seven hundred ninety-two million, eight hundred sixty-three thousand, two hundred fifty-four
- Lesson 16 worksheet
  - They can fill in the boxes using any digits except zero. Every box should be filled in and each number should be different.
- Lesson 16+ worksheet
  - They should do the first section of multiplication problems.

Lesson 17 (scissors)

- Students will: write numbers to the hundred millions in standard, expanded, and word form; practice division facts
- Lesson 17 worksheet
  - Cut out the digits and commas and make numbers together.
  - Have your child make numbers to the hundred millions. You'll need all but one of the digits to do that.
  - Have your child read the numbers out loud to you.
  - When you are ready, they can write in two numbers on the page.
- Lesson 16+ worksheet
  - They need to do the next section on the sheet.

Lesson 18

- Students will: practice multiplication facts, identify place value to the millions
- Lesson 18 worksheet
  - Take a look at it together. Go through each digit in the example and name the place value: ones, tens, hundreds, thousands, ten thousands, next would be hundred thousands, and then millions.
  - All the possible answers are at the top of the page.
- Lesson 16+ worksheet
  - They need to complete the next section.

Lesson 19

- Students will: practice division facts, write numbers in the millions in expanded form
- Lesson 19 worksheet
  - They might need to write their expanded form over two lines to fit it all in. That's okay. They need to be careful to get the correct number of zeros. One million has six zeros. Make sure they are using commas to keep the number sizes straight.
  - Have your child read to you their numbers and the other numbers on the page when they are finished.
- Lesson 16+ worksheet
  - They need to complete the next section.

Lesson 20

- Students will: practice subtraction facts, write numbers to the millions in standard, expanded, and word form
- Lesson 20 worksheet
  - They should be able to do this on their own.
- Lesson 16+ worksheet
  - They need to do the last section on the page. It's subtraction just to keep things fresh.

Mental Math

Lesson 21

- Students will: practice multiplication facts, answer mental math questions
- You are going to read the questions to them. They are not to write down the questions, only the answers. They are to solve them in their heads. Encourage your child to picture the numbers being read. Don't repeat the question for them. They need to pay attention and do the best they can. When you start the next question, they need to focus again and just move on.

- Lesson 21 worksheet
    - What number is 20 more than 40? **60**
    - What number is 30 less than 60? **30**
    - Start with 6, add 3, subtract 4. **5**
    - Start with 8, subtract 5, add 3. **6**
    - What number is halfway between 20 and 30? **25**
    - Add 40 + 6. **46**
    - Add 50 + 30. **80**
    - How many quarters are in a dollar? **4**
- Now you can re-read the list and have them share their answers for you to check.
- Mental Math Strategy
    - Break big numbers apart. Use expanded notation.
        - $583 + 344 = 500 + 80 + 3 + 300 + 40 + 4 =$
        - Add the parts: hundreds, tens, one.
        - $800 + 120 + 7 = 927$
    - Have your child try to add 317 + 568 in their head.
        - $300 + 10 + 7 + 500 + 60 + 8 = 800 + 70 + 15 = 885$
        - They could write down the end pieces as they add in their heads (eg. $800 + 70 + 15$).
- There are also facts to practice on the page. Time your child answering the facts problems. Record their time.

Lesson 22

- Students will: practice division facts, answer mental math questions
- You are going to read the questions to them. They are not to write down the questions, only the answers. They are to solve them in their heads. Don't repeat the question for them. They need to pay attention and do the best they can. When you start the next question, they need to focus again and just move on.
- Lesson 22 worksheet
    - What number is 20 more than 50? **70**
    - What number is 10 less than 40? **30**
    - Start with 9, subtract 6, add 2. **5**
    - Start with 4, add 7, subtract 9. **2**
    - What number is halfway between 60 and 70? **65**
    - What number is in the tens place in 432? **3**
    - What number is in the hundreds place in 687? **6**
    - How many dimes are in a dollar? **10**
- Now you can re-read the list and have them share their answers for you to check.
- Mental Math Strategy
    - Break big numbers apart. Use expanded notation.
        - $654 - 328 = 600 + 50 + 4 - 300 - 20 - 8 =$
            - Why did I subtract 20 and 8?
                - We're not just subtracting 300, but 328. Each part needs to get subtracted off.
            - Then you can combine the hundreds, tens, and ones.

- ▪ 300 + 30 - 4 = 326 or 300 + 20 + 6 = 326
- ▪ The first answer I gave subtracts 4 – 8 and gets – 4. See the number line below.
- ▪ The second answer borrows ten from 30 and is left with 20 and 14 – 8. They can do whatever they find easier.
  - They can practice with the number line and do 5 – 2 and 2 – 5, 7 – 4 and 4 – 7, etc. to see that the number is always the same. The only difference is if that number is being added or subtracted.

- ▪ Try one: 782 – 315 = 700 + 80 + 2 – 300 – 10 – 5 =
  - 400 + 70 – 3 = 467 or 400 + 60 + 7 = 467
- There are also facts to practice on the page. Time your child answering the facts problems. Record their time.

Lesson 23

- Students will: practice multiplication facts, answer mental math questions
- You are going to read the questions to them. They are not to write down the questions, only the answers. They are to solve them in their heads. Don't repeat the question for them. They need to pay attention and do the best they can. When you start the next question, they need to focus again and just move on.
- Lesson 23 worksheet
  - What number is 30 + 60? **90**
  - What is 80 – 40 ? **40**
  - What is 3 + 6 + 4? **13**
  - What is 5 + 5 – 6? **4**
  - Round 46 to the nearest ten. **50**
  - Round 7862 to the nearest thousand. **8000**
  - What is six tens and three ones? **63**
  - What is eight tens and five ones? **85**
- Now you can re-read the list and have them share their answers for you to check.
- Mental Math Strategy
  - Round the numbers and then adjust the answer.
    - ▪ 57 + 39… What number is 39 close to?
      - 40
      - Round 39 to 40 and then easily find the answer.
      - 57 + 40 = 97
    - ▪ But we were only supposed to add 39. We added one extra. What should we do to the answer to fix that?
      - We added one extra; we need to take that one off.
      - 97 – 1 = 96
- Continued on the next page…

10

- o Try it with subtraction. Let's use the same problem.
  - 57 – 39 rounds to 57 – 40 = 17
  - What do we need to do to fix the answer?
    - We took off one too many, so we need to add it back on.
    - 17 + 1 = 18
  - o Have your child try to solve these in their head.
    - 46 + 28 and 46 – 28
      - 28 can round to 30.
      - 46 + 30 = 76 adjust 76 – 2 = 74
      - 46 – 30 = 16 adjust 16 + 2 = 18
- There are also facts to practice on the page. Time your child answering the facts problems. Record their time.

Lesson 24

- Students will: practice division facts, answer mental math questions
- You are going to read the questions to them. They are not to write down the questions, only the answers. They are to solve them in their heads. Don't repeat the question for them. They need to pay attention and do the best they can. When you start the next question, they need to focus again and just move on.
- Lesson 24 worksheet
  - o What number is 90 - 20? **70**
  - o What 30 + 40? **70**
  - o What is 7 + 5 + 4? **16**
  - o What is 8 + 2 + 3? **13**
  - o Round 415 to the nearest hundred. **400**
  - o Round 2232 to the nearest thousand. **2000**
  - o What is 9 tens and 6 ones? **96**
  - o What is 3 hundreds, 4 tens, and 6 ones? **346**
- Now you can re-read the list and have them share their answers for you to check.
- Mental Math Strategy
  - o Easy numbers
    - Rounding makes easy numbers to add, but there are other easy numbers to add.
    - What about adding 25 + 27? Do you know what 25 + 25 is?
      - 50
      - How would you have to adjust the answer because the real question was adding 27 not 25?
        - o You'd add on two more, so the answer is 52.
  - o The important thing to remember is that you can manipulate numbers. You don't have to just line them up and add and subtract straight down. You can make them work for you.
- Continued on the next page…

- o Here's one more example. I'll solve it several ways.
  - $37 + 54 = 30 + 7 + 50 + 4 = 80 + 11 = 91$ (expanded form)
  - $37 + 53 = 80 + 10 = 90 + 1$ (adjust) $= 91$
    - $7 + 3$ add to 10 (easy numbers to add)
  - $40 + 54 = 94 - 3$ (adjust) $= 91$
- There are also facts to practice on the page. Time your child answering the facts problems. Record their time.

Lesson 25

- Students will: solve equations and word problem using mental math techniques
- Lesson 25 worksheet
  - o Encourage your child to use the techniques such as expanded notation and rounding to figure out the answers. Can they do it in their heads?

Multiplying Bigger Numbers

Lesson 26

- Students will: practice addition facts, perform mental math operations, be introduced to multiplying two digits by one digit
- Lesson 26+ worksheets
  - o Facts – They should do the first section today.
  - o Mental Math – Here are the questions. Again, don't repeat the questions. Encourage them to picture the numbers as they are being read and write down the answers as quickly as they can.
    - Of these numbers, which two make ten? 4, 5, 6 **4 + 6 = 10**
    - Add $4 + 6 + 7$. **17**
    - What number is 3 thousands, 2 hundreds? **3200**
    - What number is 4 hundreds, 5 tens, 2 ones? **452**
    - Sam has two birds, three cats, and two hamsters. How many pets does he have? **7 pets**
    - What is twenty more than sixty? **80**
    - What is twenty more than 360? **380**
    - What is ten more than 180? **190**
- Lesson 26 worksheet
  - o Multiplying
  - o Look at the examples on the page together.
    - 16 x 4 Walk through the steps and point to the numbers.
      - First you multiply the ones, 6 x 4. The answer is 24.
      - You write the 4 in the answer in the ones column, and the 2 above the tens column.
        - o This is just like when we add and get an answer greater than nine. We carry the one over to the tens column. We do the same thing with multiplication.
- Continued on the next page…

- Then you multiply by the tens, 1 x 4 = 4. We add on the 2 written on top. 4 + 2 = 6
- We write 6 in the tens column. The answer is 64.
  - 98 x 4
    - First you multiply the ones, 4 x 8 = 32.
    - You write the two in the ones column and the three in the tens column up top.
    - Then you multiply four by the tens. 4 x 9 = 36.
    - You already have three in the tens column, so you add that on. 36 + 3 = 39.
    - You write 39 in the tens place. The 3 will carry over into the hundreds column. There's nothing else there to add it to, so it goes straight into the answer.
    - The answer is 392.
- o Have your child write down the steps as you read through the first line of problems.
  - 41 x 3
    - Multiply three times the ones, 1 x 3. They will write the answer in the ones place.
    - Then multiply three times the tens, 4 x 3. They will write the answer in the tens place. There are 12 tens. It will "spill over" into the hundreds column. We'd add it onto whatever number is there, but this time there are no other numbers in the hundreds place.
      - o Twelve tens is one hundred and twenty. (They can count by tens twelve times to be sure if they want.)
    - The answer is 123.
  - 41 x 30 This is very similar to what we just did.
    - There are zero ones. Anything times zero is just zero. They should write the answer to 41 x 0 in the ones column for the answer.
    - Now they will multiply 3 times the ones.
      - o Multiply 3 times the ones, 3 x 1 = 3.
      - o They will write that answer in the tens column.
        - This makes sense. So far they've really just multiplied 30 x 1, which is just 30. Their answer is 30 so far.
      - o Multiply 3 times the 4, 3 x 4 = 12.
        - They will write this in the next column in the answer.
          - This makes sense because it's not really 3 x 4 we're multiplying. We're multiplying 30 x 40.
        - The one can carry over, but there's nothing to add it onto, so it can just go in the answer.
      - o The answer is 1230.

- 27 x 5
  - Twenty-seven is 20 + 7. We multiply each part by the five.
  - Multiply five by the ones. 5 x 7 = 35
  - Write the 5 in the ones column. The 3 will "spill over" but we have to write it in the column, not in the answer.
    - This is just like when we add and get an answer over nine. We write the ones in the ones column and then write a little one above the tens column.
  - Now multiply the 5 times the tens. 5 x 2 = 10. We need to add on the three tens in the column. 10 + 3 = 13.
  - Write 13 in the tens column.
  - The answer is 135.
  - Today, they will just be multiplying by one digit.
    - They will multiply it by the ones and write the answer in the ones place, carrying into the tens column if they need to.
    - Then they will multiply by the tens and write the answer in the tens column. The answer might spill over into the hundreds.

Lesson 27

- Students will: practice division facts, perform mental math operations, be introduced to multiplying two digits by two digits
- Lesson 26+ worksheets
  - Facts – They should do the next section today.
  - Mental Math – Here are the questions. Again, don't repeat the questions. Encourage them to picture the numbers as they are being read and write down the answers as quickly as they can.
    - Which two of these numbers make ten? 3, 5, 7 **3 + 7 =10**
    - Add five plus three plus seven. **15**
    - What number is in the hundreds place in 3642? **6**
    - What number is 6 hundreds and 2 ones? **602**
    - Sarah has 4 red stamps, 6 blue, and 7 green. How many stamps does she have? **17 stamps**
    - What is 30 + 40? **70**
    - What is 20 + 130? **150**
    - What is 40 + 410? **450**
- Lesson 27 worksheet
  - Multiply.
  - Go through the example together.
    - 78 x 20
      - 78 x 0 is just zero.
        - You write zero in the answer in the ones column.
- Continued on the next page…

- Then you multiply 2 by the ones.
  - 8 x 2 = 16
    - You write six in the next column and carry the one.
- Then you multiply the 2 by the tens.
  - 7 x 2 = 14
  - Add on the one. 14 + 1 = 15
    - You write the 5 in the next column and carry the one but there's nothing to add it to. One plus nothing is just one, so that's what goes next in the answer.
- The answer is 1560.
  - 41 x 23
    - What's 23 in expanded form?
      - 20 + 3
    - This problem is really 41 x 20 plus 41 x 3. That's what we're going to do. Multiply 41 by each part, and then add the answers together. They already know how to multiply those pieces.
    - Start with 41 x 3.
      - Have your child write the steps as you read through them.
      - Multiply 3 by the ones.
        - 3 x 1 = 3
          - Write that in the ones column.
      - Multiply 3 by the tens.
        - 3 x 4 = 12
          - Write the 2 in the next column.
          - You carry the one to the next column but there's nothing to add it to. It can just go straight into the answer.
      - That's our first answer. We'll write our next answer below that, so that we can add them together when we're done.
        - 123
    - 41 x 20
      - Zero times 41 is 0. We can just write 0 in the ones column. This will go under the 3 you already have there.
      - Now multiply the 2 by the ones.
        - 2 x 1 = 2
          - Write that in the next column in your answer.
- Continued on the next page…

- o Finally, multiply the 2 by the 4.
  - ▪ 2 x 4 = 8
    - • Write that in the next column.
- o The answer to that part is 820.
- • The last step is to add together your two answers. The one answer is 41 times 20 and the other is 41 times 3. You want to know how much is 41 times 23 times, so we put the answers together.
  - o 123 + 820 = 943
- ▪ 27 x 65
  - • Have your child write the steps as you read through them. Give them time to answer the multiplication problems before you tell them.
  - • 65 = 60 + 5 This problem is 27 x 60 plus 27 x 5.
- ▪ Multiply 27 x 5.
  - • Start with the ones. 5 x 7 = 35
    - o Write in the answer and carry the three up to the tens column.
  - • Now multiply the 5 by the tens. 5 x 2 = 10.
    - o Add on the three from the tens column and write in the answer of 13 tens.
      - ▪ Cross off the three after you've added it.
    - o That's the problem we did on Lesson 26.
  - • Now we have to add that answer to the answer of 27 x 60.
- ▪ Multiply 27 by 60.
  - • Start with the ones. 27 x 0 = 0.
    - o Write 0 in a new row. Zero goes in the ones column.
  - • Now take the tens, the 6, and multiply it by 27.
    - o Start with the ones. 7 x 6 = 42
      - ▪ Write 2 in the next column (the tens) and carry the 4. Write it on top of the two.
    - o Next, multiply it by the tens. 2 x 6 = 12
    - o Add on the 4.
      - ▪ Cross off any number after you add it on.
    - o Write the answer in the next column, the hundreds.
      - ▪ It will "spill over" into the thousands.
- ▪ The final step is to add together the answers to 27 x 5 and 27 x 60.
- ▪ The answer is 1755.
- • Continued on the next page…

- 26 x 35
  - What's 35 in expanded form?
    - 30 + 5
    - This problem is 26 x 5 plus 26 x 30.
  - Start with 26 x 5.
    - Start with the ones.
      - 6 x 5 = 30
        - Write zero in the ones place and carry the three.
    - Next multiply by the tens.
      - 2 x 5 = 10
      - Add on what was carried and cross it off.
        - 10 + 3 = 13
      - Write 3 in the next column and carry the one over into the next column in the answer.
    - The answer to this part is 130.
  - Now multiply 26 x 30.
    - We automatically start the next row's answer with a zero in the ones column. 26 x 0 = 0
    - Then we multiply 3 x 26, starting with the ones.
      - 3 x 6 = 18
        - 8 goes in the next column in the answer and the 1 is carried over.
    - Then we multiply the tens.
      - 3 x 2 = 6
      - Add the one that was carried and cross it off.
        - 6 + 1 = 7 and write that in the next column in the answer.
    - The answer to this part is 780.
  - The last step is to add your answers.
    - 130 + 780 = 910
  - We'll be practicing this over the next few days.
  - There are four more problems on the sheet for them to try on their own. Encourage them to use the examples you just did together.

Lesson 28

- Students will: practice subtraction facts, perform mental math operations, multiply two digits by two digits
- Lesson 26+ worksheets
  - Facts – They should do the next section today.
  - Mental Math – Here are the questions. Don't repeat them. Have them write their answers; then you can go back through and repeat them and give them the answers to check.

- Start with 300 and write the next five numbers.
  - **301, 302, 303, 304, 305**
- Write all of the even numbers between 30 and 40.
  - **32, 34, 36, 38**
- What is 30 more than 120? **150**
- What is 50 less than 170? **120**
- What is halfway between 100 and 200? **150**
- Add 6 + 3 + 7. **16** (3 + 7 = 10)
- Add 3 + 8 + 2. **13** (8 + 2 = 10)
- What is halfway between 1000 and 2000? **1500**
- Lesson 28 worksheet
  - Multiplying two-digit numbers
    - They can look back at Lesson 27 if they want to look at examples.
    - They are going to think about the one number being in expanded form and then multiplying each part by the other number.

Lesson 29

- Students will: practice division facts, perform mental math operations, multiply two digits by two digits
- Lesson 26+ worksheets
  - Facts – They should do the next section today.
  - Mental Math – Here are the questions. Don't repeat them. Have them write their answers. Then you can go back through and repeat them and give them the answers to check.
    - Start with 1000. Write the next five numbers.
      - **1001, 1002, 1003, 1004, 1005**
    - Write all the odd numbers between 50 and 60.
      - **51, 53, 55, 57, 59**
    - What is 210 + 60? **270**
    - What is 190 – 40? **150**
    - What is halfway between 300 and 400? **350**
    - What is halfway between 2000 and 3000? **2500**
    - Add 8 + 5 + 5? **18** (5 +5 = 10)
    - Add 9 + 7 + 3? **19** (7 + 3 = 10)
- Lesson 29 worksheet
  - Multiplying two-digit numbers
    - They can look back at previous days if they want to look at examples.
    - They are going to think about the one number being in expanded form and then multiplying each part by the other number.

Lesson 30

- Students will: write numbers in standard and expanded form; round numbers to the nearest ten, hundred, and thousand; calculate the total value of a group of bills and coins
- Lesson 30 worksheet
    - This is a review page.
    - When they are rounding (Part B), they need to pay attention to what place value they are working with. If you want to review it with them, here's a number to practice with.
        - 3245
            - To the nearest 10: look at the ones, 5, and round up
                - 3250
            - To the nearest 100: look at the tens, 4, and round down
                - 3200
            - To the nearest 1000: look at the hundreds, 2 and round down
                - 3000

Graphs and Charts

Lesson 31

- Students will: practice addition facts, perform mental math operations, create bar graphs and a pictograph
- Lesson 31+ Mental Math Worksheet
    - Read each only once. Then read through it again and check answers.
        - What number is in the tens place in 732? **3**
        - What number is in the tens place in 506? **0**
        - How much is twelve tens? **120   12x10**
        - How much is 26 tens? **260   26x10**
        - I'm thinking of a number between 20 and 40. It has a five in it? What number could it be? **25 or 35**
        - Add 13 + 4. **17**
        - Add 24 + 5. **29**
        - Add 62 + 8. **70   notice 2+8=10 then 10+60=70**
- Lesson 31 worksheet
    - I think the best way to approach this is to look at the worksheet together. There are two pages. The second page is to create your own graph. Start with the first page.
        - Look at the tally-mark chart. What does it show?
            - It shows how many coins were collected by each child.
        - Ask your child how they would show that on the bar graph and pictograph.
- Continued on the next page…

- On the bar graph, they would fill in a block for each number. Ron's column would be filled to the top.
  - Point out the labels along the bottom and side and the title at the top.
    - They will need to use labels and a title on their own graph.
- On the pictograph, they would draw one coin for every two coins collected. To show Max's five coins, they would draw two whole coins and one half coin. (2+2+1=5).
  - After they fill out the first page, they need to come up with their own idea to graph.
    - They could do colors of things in the room, how many letters people have in their first name, people's favorite day of the week, favorite foods, etc.
      - There are five categories to fill in and tally.
    - Then they need to translate that information onto the graph.
- Lesson 31+ worksheet (facts)
  - They should do the first section on the page.

Lesson 32 (6 colors of crayons/pencils/thin markers)

- Students will: practice multiplication facts, create line and circle graphs, perform mental math operations
- Lesson 31+ worksheets
  - Facts – Do the next section on the page.
  - Mental Math – Read each one time and allow them to answer before moving on.
    - What number is in the hundreds place in 5822? **8**
    - What number is in the hundreds place in 6032? **0**
    - How much is 16 tens? **160 16x10**
    - How much is 34 hundreds? **3400 34x100**
    - Add 36 + 3. **39**
    - Add 83 + 7. **90 notice that 3+7=10 and 10+80=90**
    - Add 26 + 4. **30 notice that 6+ 4=10 and 10+20=30**
    - Tim had 40 pages in his notebook. He tore out 10. How many are left? **30 pages**
- Lesson 32 worksheet
  - Look at the first table. Have your child see what it's saying.
    - It's showing how many cups of lemonade were sold each day of the week.
    - They are to plot those points on the graph.
      - Monday is 5 cups. They need to find where the lines for Monday and 5 intersect and put a dot there.
- Continued on the next page…

- Then they will connect the dots left to right.
  - This clearly shows how the number of sales is increasing or decreasing from day to day and over time.
- Look at the second chart. Ask your child how they will fill it in to show how much money was spent on each item?
  - They will color each box in a different color.
  - They will color the number of "slices" that matches the number of dollars.
    - For lemons, they might color the box in yellow. Then they would color 9 slices yellow to show that $9 was spent on lemons.

Lesson 33

- Students will: practice subtraction facts, perform mental math operations, answer graphing questions
- Lesson 31+ worksheets
  - Facts – Do the next section on the page.
  - Mental Math – Read each one time and allow them to answer before moving on.
    - Make the largest number you can with 1, 2, and 3. **321**
    - Make the smallest number you can with 1, 2, and 3. **123**
    - Round 36 to the nearest ten. **40**
    - Round 81 to the nearest ten. **80**
    - Add 3 + 9 + 7. **19**
    - What is 10 + 16? **26**
    - What is 20 + 32? **52**
    - Maria had $10. She spent $2 on pencils and $1 on candy. How much money does she have left? **$7**
- Lesson 33 worksheet
  - Frequency diagrams are another way of naming all the different things they've been using: tables, charts, and graphs. They show the frequency of things, how often, how much, etc.
  - The questions are about all different kinds of graphs and how they would be used and read.

Lesson 34

- Students will: practice division facts, perform mental math operations, read a double line graph
- Lesson 31+ worksheets
  - Facts – Do the next section on the page.
  - Mental Math – Read each one time and allow them to answer before moving on.

- Round 85 to the nearest ten. **90**
- Round 618 to the nearest hundred. **600**
- Add 4 + 9 + 6. **19 notice 4+6=10**
- What is 20 + 56? **76**
- What is 20 + 256? **276**
- What is 40 + 120? **160**
- How many nickels are in a dollar? **20**
- How many nickels are in two dollars? **40, double 20**
- Lesson 34 worksheet
  - A double line graph is used to compare two different things. Ask your child what the graph shows and what is being compared.
    - It's showing how much money was spent each month and compares how much each girl spent.
  - They will use the graph to answer the questions.
    - For the last one, they don't have to add up all the amounts. They could just compare the two by looking at the points along the graph. For instance, follow Olivia and compare her to Abby.
      - She's up two and then comes down one making her up one still. Then she is down two putting her down one compared to Abby, etc.

Lesson 35

- Students will: practice facts, review coin math and reading analog clocks
- Lesson 35 worksheet
  - Make sure your child knows the value of the coins.
  - Make sure your child can read the clocks with no numbers on them. Each line is counting by five around the clock.
- Lesson 31+ worksheet

Multiplying Bigger Numbers

Lesson 36

- Students will: practice addition facts, perform mental math operations, multiply one and two digits by three digits
- Lesson 36+ worksheets
  - Facts – Do the first section on the page.
  - Mental Math – Read each one time and allow them to answer before moving on.
    - Write the even numbers between 230 and 240.
      - **232, 234, 236, 238**
    - Write the odd numbers between 450 and 460.
      - **451, 453, 455, 457, 459**
    - What is 200 + 426? **626**
    - What is 400 + 210? **610**
    - What is 20 + 150? **170**

- What is 40 + 620? **660**
- Add 26 + 20. **46**
- How much greater is 70 than 40? **30**

- Lesson 36 worksheet
  - Walk through the first example together, 875 x 6.
    - They multiply the 6 times the ones, the 5, and put that in the ones place in the answer.
      - If it's too much, they carry it over to the next column and write it above the tens column.
      - They will write a three above the seven.
    - They multiply the 6 times the tens, the 7, and add it to what was carried over and put that in the tens place.
      - Once they add on the three, they should cross it off.
      - The four will get carried into the hundreds column.
    - Then they multiply 6 times the hundreds, the 8, and add what was carried over.
      - They should cross off the four after they add it on.
      - The answer goes in the hundreds place, letting it spill over into the thousands column because there's nothing there to add it to.
  - Let your child work on the next two problems.
    - They are crossing off what they carry after they add it because when you multiply by two digits (or more) there can be multiple numbers carried on top. Crossing them off helps keep it straight.
    - 616 x 4 = 2464
  - Walk through the example with two digits, 411 x 56.
    - What's 56 in expanded form?
      - 50 + 6
    - That's what you are multiplying by. You are multiplying 411 x 6 and adding it to 411 x 50.
    - You start with 411 x 6.
      - 2,466
    - Then they will multiply 411 x 50.
      - 411 x 0 is just zero, so they write 0 in the ones place on the next line.
      - Then they multiply 411 x 5.
        - 20,550
    - The last step is to add them together.
      - 23,016
  - Have your child try the last problem on the first line while you watch and help talk through the steps if necessary.
  - Then they can try the rest of the page.
    - Have them go back and fix any mistakes.

Lesson 37

- Students will: practice multiplication facts, perform mental math operations, multiply one and two digits by three digits
- Lesson 36+ worksheets
  - Facts – Do the next section on the page. This is multiplication which they are doing anyway, so they should focus on doing them quickly.
  - Mental Math – Read each one time and allow them to answer before moving on.
    - Make the largest number you can out of 2, 4 and 6. **642**
    - What number is in the tens place in 4000? **0**
    - What is 50 + 610? **660**
    - What is 90 – 40? **50**
    - What is 540 – 20? **520**
    - What is 670 – 40? **630**
    - Subtract 20 from 78? **58**
    - Start with 9 subtract 5 add 4 add 3 subtract 2. **9**
- Lesson 37 worksheet
  - Walk through the example together, 475 x 381.
    - What is 381 in expanded form?
      - 300 + 80 + 1
      - That's what they are multiplying by.
      - They are going to multiply 475 times 1, 475 times 80, and 475 x 300 and add them all together.
    - First the ones. 475 x 1.
      - They know how to do this. The first line's answer is 475.
    - Then the tens, multiplying by 80.
      - 475 x 0 is zero, so zero is written in the ones column on the next line (under the 5).
      - It's important to write each answer in the correct column to help them add in the end.
      - 475 x 8 is next. Multiply across the row, ones, tens, hundreds, carrying and adding and writing each answer in the next column.
    - Then the hundreds, multiplying by 300.
      - 475 x 0 is zero and 475 x 0 is zero, so the first two answers we write are two zeros in the ones and tens place on the next line.
      - Then we just have the hundreds left to multiply by.
        - Multiply 3 across the row, ones, tens, hundreds.
        - They should be careful to write each number in the answer in the next column so that they add correctly at the end.
    - The last step is to add all three answers together.
  - There are three types of problems on the page, but they are all tackled the same way.

Lesson 38

- Students will: practice subtraction facts, perform mental math operations, multiply three digits by three digits
- Lesson 36+ worksheets
  - Facts – Do the next section on the page.
  - Mental Math – Read each one time and allow them to answer before moving on.
    - How many dimes in two quarters? **5**
    - How many nickels in two quarters? **10**
    - What time is thirty minutes after five o'clock? **5:30**
    - What time is thirty minutes after 5:15? **5:45**
    - What number is 8 hundreds and 4 tens? **840**
    - What number is 3 hundreds and 4 tens? **340**
    - What is $16 + 4$? **20**
    - What is $16 + 5$? **21 Mental math strategy: You know $16 + 4$. 5 is one more than 4, so the answer will be one more.**
- Lesson 38 worksheet
  - When they are finished, they should have their answers checked and they should fix or redo any problems with mistakes.

Lesson 39

- Students will: practice division facts, perform mental math operations, multiply three digits by three digits
- Lesson 36+ worksheets
  - Facts – Do the next section on the page.
  - Mental Math – Read each one time and allow them to answer before moving on.
    - Make the smallest number you can with 8, 1, 4 and 5. **1458**
    - How many nickels in three dimes? **6**
    - What time is 30 minutes after three o'clock? **3:30**
    - What number is 3 hundreds and 5 ones? **305**
    - What number is 2 thousands, 3 tens, and 7 ones? **2037**
    - Add $37 + 3$. **40**
    - Add $37 + 5$. **42 5 is two more, so the answer is two more.**
- Lesson 39 worksheet
  - When they are finished, they should have their answers checked, and they should fix or redo any problems with mistakes.

Lesson 40

- Students will: practice facts, read a data table, round thousands to the nearest ten, hundred, and thousand; convert numbers from expanded form to standard form
- Lesson 36+ worksheet
    - Facts – Do the last section on the page.
- Lesson 40 worksheet
    - These are review activities. They should be able to complete this without any lesson.

Lesson 41

- Students will: practice addition facts, perform mental math operations, multiply one digit by two digits
- Lesson 41+ worksheets
    - Facts – Do the first section on the page.
    - Mental Math – Read each one time and allow them to answer before moving on.
        - Practice with this first: add 15 + 7. They can think about expanding 15. Into what? 10 + 5. What's 10 + 5 + 7. They can just add 5 + 7 and then easily add on the 10.
            - Have them try one on their own using this method.
                - $13 + 8 = 10 + 3 + 8 = 10 + 11 = 21$
                - This keeps them from having to think about carrying in their heads.
        - How much is 38 tens? **380**
        - How much is 14 hundreds? **1400**
        - How much is 56 thousands? **56,000**
        - Add 16 + 7. **23**
        - Add 18 + 5. **23**
        - Subtract 46 – 20. **26**
        - Subtract 78 – 30. **48**
        - Michael had 38 markers. He gave 20 of them to Matt. How many markers does he have left? **18 markers**
- Lesson 41 worksheet
    - When they are finished, they should have their answers checked, and they should fix or redo any problems with mistakes.
    - They are going to be building up over the week towards 3 digit by 3 digit multiplication, so be sure they get each step along the way.

Lesson 42

- Students will: practice multiplication facts, perform mental math operations, multiply two digits by two digits
- Lesson 41+ worksheets
    - Facts – Do the next section on the page. This is multiplication, which they are going to be practicing on their worksheet, but the focus of the facts page is to be quick about it.
    - Mental Math – Read each one time and allow them to answer before moving on.
        - First practice with this: 88 + 8. Can you think of some ways you could break up those number to make them easier to add?
            - Here are two ideas.
                - 80 + 8 + 8 = 80 + 16 = 96
                - 88 + 2 + 6 = 90 + 6 = 96
            - You try it on your own with 77 + 8.
                - 70 + 7 + 8 = 70 + 15 = 85
                - 77 + 3 + 5 = 80 + 5 = 85
        - Write the number that is 5 ones and 4 tens. **45**
        - Write the number that is 3 hundreds, 7 tens, and 2 ones. **372**
        - Start with 3, add 4, add 3, add 6. **16**
        - Which numbers make ten from 2, 7, and 8? **2+8**
        - What is 30 + 60? **90**
        - What number is halfway between 50 and 70? **60**
        - What is 80 – 40? **40**
        - What is 38 + 20? **58**
- Lesson 42 worksheet
    - When they are finished, they should have their answers checked, and they should fix or redo any problems with mistakes.

Lesson 43

- Students will: practice subtraction facts, perform mental math operations, multiply three digits by two digits
- Lesson 41+ worksheets
    - Facts – Do the next section on the page.
    - Mental Math – Read each one time and allow them to answer before moving on.
        - Practice first:
            - What's 27 + 3?
                - 7 + 3 = 10
                - 20 + 10 = 30
            - Try one more on your own.
                - What's 16 + 4?
                    - 6 + 4 = 10
                    - 10 + 10 = 20

- How many dimes in 50 cents? **5**
- What is 45 + 5? **50 5 + 5 = 10, 40 + 10 = 50**
- What is 3 more than 7? **10**
- What number is halfway between 10 and 20? **15**
- Write any number that has three in the tens place. **30, varies**
- What is 22 + 8 + 30? **60 2 + 8 = 10, 20 + 10 + 30 = 60**
- What is ten less than forty? **30**
- What is ten more than 615? **625**
- Lesson 43 worksheet
  - When they are finished, they should have their answers checked, and they should fix or redo any problems with mistakes.

Lesson 44

- Students will: practice division facts, perform mental math operations, multiply three digits by three digits
- Lesson 41+ worksheets
  - Facts – Do the next section on the page.
  - Mental Math – Read each one time and allow them to answer before moving on.
    - First practice with this:
      - What's 40 – 6?
        - Since forty ends in zero, think what 10 – 6 is.
          - 4
        - When we take 4 away from 40, we'll end up with 30 something. You know that from learning to borrow and regroup.
        - The answer is 34.
      - Try this on your own. What's 70 – 5?
        - 10 – 5 = 5
        - 70 – 5 = 65
    - How much money is ten nickels? **50 cents**
    - What is 88 + 8? **96**
    - What is 20 – 3? **17**
    - Start with 10, add 4, subtract 7, add 3. **10**
    - How many groups of three are in fifteen? **5**
    - What addition fact goes with 9 – 3 = 6? **3 + 6 = 9 or 6 + 3 = 9**
    - What is two plus eight? **10**
    - Which two numbers make ten from these: 1, 7, and 9? **1 + 9 = 10**
- Lesson 44 worksheet
  - When they are finished, they should have their answers checked, and they should fix or redo any problems with mistakes.

Lesson 45

- Students will: round numbers to the nearest ten, hundred, thousand; use estimation to solve multiplication problems, practice facts
- Lesson 41+ worksheet
  - Practice the facts for speed. They need to pay attention to the sign.
- Lesson 45 worksheet
  - Look at the first one together.
    - Round 458 to the nearest hundred.
      - They will look at the number before it, the tens, and decide if that rounds up or down.
        - Five rounds up.
      - 500 is the answer.
    - Round 34 to the nearest ten.
      - They will look at the number before it, the ones, and decide if that rounds up or down.
        - Four rounds down.
      - 30
    - Then they multiply 500 by 30.
      - To do that they just multiply five times three and then add on the number of zeros in the problem.
        - There are three zeros in 500 and 30, so the answer is 15 with three zeros.
        - 15,000
  - They can complete the rest of the worksheet on their own. They just need to pay attention to how many zeros they are putting on the answer.
    - If that was 500 x 40, it would be 20 with three zeros.
    - 20,000
    - There would be four zeros in the answer.

Lesson 46

- Students will: practice addition facts, perform mental math operations, multiply three digits by two digits, solve multiplication problems by estimation
- Lesson 46+ worksheets
  - Facts – Do the first section on the page.
  - Mental Math – Read each one time and allow them to answer before moving on.
    - What is 6 thousands, 3 hundreds, and 2 tens? **6320**
    - What is 5 + 4 + 3? **12**
    - Write the next three numbers: 97, 98, 99. **100, 101, 102**
    - Write a number that has nine in the hundreds place? **900, varies**
    - What is 90 – 70? **20**
    - Nine plus what equals twelve? **3**
    - What is the thousand's place in 8643? **8**
    - Susan bought some stickers. She used five and has six left. How many did she buy? **11 stickers**

Lesson 46 worksheet

- o They need to do each problem fully and then by estimation. They need to write those two answers at the bottom of the page and find the difference between the actual and estimated answers.

Word Problems

Lesson 47

- Students will: practice multiplication facts, perform mental math operations, solve word problems
- Lesson 46+ worksheets
  - o Facts – Do the next section on the page. This is multiplication, which they are going to be practicing on their worksheet, but the focus of the facts page is to be quick about it.
  - o Mental Math – Read each one time and allow them to answer before moving on.
    - How many days are in a week? **7**
    - What is 10 + 7 – 4? **13**
    - Write the next three numbers: 46, 47, 48. **49, 50, 51**
    - What is 7 thousands, 4 hundreds, and 6 ones? **7406**
    - What is 462 + 30? **492**
    - Start with 6, add 6, add 2, add 4, add 1. **19**
    - What number is in the tens places in 8451? **5**
    - What is 600 – 10? **590**
- Practice with some word problems.
  - o Picture a group of people sitting in rows. If there were five rows and four people in each row, how many people were there?
    - You could draw a picture, you could count up the people, but the best way to answer the question is to multiply. 4 x 5 = 20
- Lesson 47 worksheet
  - o Make sure they label their answers, for instance, 20 people.

Lesson 48

- Students will: practice subtraction facts, perform mental math operations, solve word problems
- Lesson 46+ worksheets
  - o Facts – Do the next section on the page.
  - o Mental Math – Read each one time and allow them to answer before moving on.
    - Write any number that has 6 in the ones place? **6, varies**
    - What is 7 + 5 + 2? **14**
    - How many minutes are in one hour? **60**
    - What is 164 + 20? **184**
    - 400 – 100 – 30? **270**
    - What number is halfway between 0 and 10? **5**

- What number is 9 thousands and 5 ones? **9005**
- Bill has 2 brown dogs, 3 white dogs, 1 black dog, and 5 rabbits. How many dogs does Bill have? **6 dogs**
- Try a practice word problem together.
  - Each small crayon box can hold six crayons. He has 12 red crayons, 8 blue crayons, 4 green crayons, and 6 yellow crayons. How many boxes can be filled with crayons?
    - It needs to be done in parts. Add together the number of crayons and then divide by six.
      - 30 crayons divided by 6 equals 5 boxes
      - Make sure to label your answer.
- Lesson 48 worksheet
  - Encourage them to use a picture or smaller numbers if they are ever lost about what to do. And require them to label their answers!

Lesson 49

- Students will: practice division facts, perform mental math operations, solve word problems using multiplication and division
- Lesson 46+ worksheets
  - Facts – Do the next section on the page.
  - Mental Math – Read each one time and allow them to answer before moving on.
    - What time is thirty minutes after 12:10? **12:40**
    - $16 + 4 + 7$? **27**
    - What number is halfway between 30 and 40? **35**
    - Estimate the answer to $48 + 37$. **$50 + 40 = 90$**
    - About how much is $53 - 32$? **$50 - 30 = 20$**
    - What is $97 - 40$? **57**
    - How many nines in 45? **5**
    - Write a number with 2 in the tens place. **20, varies**
- Practice with these word problems.
  - I have twice the number of pets as Bruce has, and Zoe had three times the number of pets that I have. If Zoe has 12 pets, how many does Bruce have?
    - Take it in parts. Zoe has three times the number of pets as me. She has 12. How many do I have?
      - 12 divided by 3 is 4. (Or, what times 3 equals 12?)
    - Then I have twice the number Bruce has.
      - 2 times what equals 4? Or, 4 divided by 2.
        - 2 pets
    - Make sure to label your answers.

- You can check to see if you were correct to multiply or divide by rereading the question and making sure that the person who's supposed to have the most does. If not, you probably multiplied when you were supposed to divide.
- Lesson 49 worksheet
  - They need to answer the questions. Encourage them to use a picture if necessary and to label the answers!

Lesson 50

- Students will: practice facts for speed, solve word problems using multiplication and division
- Practice with these problems:
  - If you spent $20 on tickets and each ticket was $4, how many tickets did you buy?
    - You would need to divide. Four goes into twenty five times. You bought five tickets.
    - If they are ever stuck, have them draw a picture. 20 lines could be 20 dollars. They would circle four of them. With those four dollars they bought one ticket, and so on.
  - If I had three times as many marbles as you, and I have 15 marbles, how many do you have?
    - 3 times what equals 15? That's the same as 15 divided by 3.
      - 5 marbles
- Lesson 46+ worksheet
  - Practice facts.
- Lesson 50 worksheet
  - Solve the word problems. Use pictures as necessary.

Fractions

Lesson 51

- Students will: be introduced to equivalent fractions, find equivalent fractions
- Here's the lesson from EP on equivalent fractions.
  - One half, 1/2, is the same as two fourths, 2/4. What else is it the same as? If you had a pizza with 8 slices and you ate half, how many slices did you eat? 4! Four is half of eight. One way to read fractions is 4 out of 8.
  - These are all the same amount.
    - one half
    - five tenths
    - five out of ten
    - 0.5
    - 50%
    - 1/2 , 2/4 , 3/6 , 4/8 , 5/10
      - Those fractions are called **equivalent fractions**.

- o Equivalent means equal. Those fractions are all one half. The top number is half of the bottom number. The denominator is two times the numerator.
- o When we change an equivalent fraction to its lowest terms, it's called **simplifying or reducing** the fraction. That just means we take $^5/_{10}$ (five tenths) and call it $^1/_2$ (one half). If you ate 5 out of the 10 cookies, you ate one half of them. $^5/_{10}$ and $^1/_2$ are the same amount.
- o One way to find an equivalent fraction is to multiply or divide the top and bottom numbers (the numerator and the denominator) by the same amount.
- • Before we get to that, take a piece of paper and demonstrate the lesson.
  - o Have your child fold it in half and quickly scribble over half of it to color it in. They can open it and see that they have colored in half.
  - o Have your child fold the paper back in half and then fold it in half again to divide it into four parts.
    - ▪ Ask your child how much is colored in. One half is colored but so are two of the four squares, two fourths.
  - o Have your child fold up the paper again and then fold it in half one more time.
    - ▪ Now have your child tell you how much is colored in.
      - • one half, two fourths, four eighths
  - o You can try one more time folding it to make sixteen squares. Eight sixteenths will be colored in.
  - o The amount colored in never changed. It's always equal. Only how they described it changed. Equivalent fractions are all equal to each other.
- • Lesson 51 worksheet
  - o The top part is like what you just did. They can use the pictures to help them figure out equivalent fractions.
  - o In the second part they will follow the arrows to multiply and divide to make equivalent fractions.
    - ▪ Why does that work?
      - • $^2/_2$ is equal to one. $^5/_5$ is equal to one. When you have all the parts of something you have one whole. When you multiply or divide by one, you get the same number. It doesn't change. That's why multiplying and dividing by the same number on the top and bottom gives you an equivalent, equal, answer.

Lesson 52

- • Students will: find equivalent fractions, identify fractions from pictures
- • Together take a look at the Lesson 51 worksheet.
  - o They will be writing equivalent fractions from pictures and multiplying or dividing to find the equivalent fractions (but without the guiding arrows).
  - o Make sure they understand this worksheet before they start working on Lesson 52's page.

- Lesson 52 worksheet
  - They will be practicing equivalent fractions.
  - For the first section they need to write in the numerator based on the number of blocks colored in. Then they need think about how to get to the new number of pieces. They can draw lines on the picture to help. They could also think about what to multiply the first denominator by to get to the second denominator and then multiply the top by the same number.
    - It will always be two or three on this page.
  - For the second section, they will be multiplying the numerator and denominator by either two or three to find the equivalent fraction.

Lesson 53

- Students will: compare fractions with like and unlike denominators
- Ask your child what they write to show which is greater, 61 or 59.
  - 61 > 59
  - We use the greater than/less than symbol and the small end points to the smaller number and the big end points to the bigger number.
- Ask your child which is bigger, one third or two thirds?
  - Two thirds is bigger.
  - They could draw a simple picture to show that if they aren't confident. They just need to compare the numerators because they are comparing numbers with the same number of pieces.
- Ask your child which is bigger one half or four eighths?
  - They are equal. Even though four is bigger than one, we're talking about different numbers of pieces. When they folded the paper in half and in half, we showed that one half equaled four eighths.
  - You can't compare fractions unless they have an equal number of pieces.
- Ask your child which is bigger, one half or two fifths?
  - What do they need to do?
    - They need to give them an equal number of pieces before they can compare.
  - 1/2 is greater than 2/5 because…
  - 1/2 equals 5/10 (multiply top and bottom by 5)
  - 2/5 equals 4/10 (multiply top and bottom by 2)
  - 5 > 4
  - So, one half is greater than two fifths.
- Lesson 53 worksheet
  - To find the largest fraction they should eliminate what they know can't be right.
    - For instance if there was $3/6$ and $6/9$, they could see that three sixths is one half and six ninth is bigger than one half since six is half of twelve.
    - What's bigger $3/5$ or $3/9$?
      - Three fifths is bigger because there are the same number of pieces and something divided into fifths has bigger pieces.

34

Lesson 54

- Students will: add and subtract fractions with like denominators
- Lesson 54 worksheet
  - Take a look at the example word problem together.
    - When they add one quarter plus one quarter plus one quarter, the number of pieces doesn't change. They just need to add the numerators. The denominator will stay the same.
  - When they look at the egg example, the total number of eggs the carton can hold doesn't change, only the number of eggs used changes. The denominator will stay the same and the numerator will change.
  - They only need to add or subtract the numbers in the numerator.

Lesson 55

- Students will: identify proper fractions and reciprocals
- A **proper** fraction is when the numerator is less than the denominator.
  - Is two thirds a proper fraction?
    - yes
  - Is five fourths a proper fraction?
    - no
  - Is two halves a proper fraction?
    - no, 2 is not less than 2
- Lesson 55 worksheet
  - They need to carefully read the directions. In the first part they are looking for proper fractions, but in the second part they are looking for ones that aren't proper. In the third section the sum or difference of the numerators needs to be less than the denominator.

Lesson 56

- Students will: identify improper fractions and their reciprocals
- We learned about proper fractions. When a fraction isn't proper, it's called an **improper fraction**.
  - Ask your child to tell you what they think the definition of an improper fraction is. What makes a fraction improper? (Besides not being proper!)
    - An improper fraction is one where the numerator is greater than or equal to the denominator.
- Ask your child what a reciprocal of an improper fraction would be?
  - A reciprocal is the fraction flipped upside down where the numerator and denominator switch places.
  - It would be a proper fraction.
- Lesson 56 worksheet
  - This is set up like the Lesson 55 worksheet. They need to pay attention to the directions.

Lesson 57

- Students will: identify mixed numbers, convert improper fractions to mixed numbers
- A **mixed number** (some call it a mixed fraction) is a whole number together with a fraction.
- There's a place on the worksheet to practice this.
- Lesson 57 worksheet
  - Use the "Make mixed numbers" top section together.
  - Have your child divide the first circle into quarters.
  - Have your child color in one quarter and write the fraction it shows under the circle.
    - ¼
  - Have them color in each quarter and tell you the fraction that is colored in.
    - two quarters (or ½), three quarters, four quarters
    - Ask your child what kind of fraction is four quarters.
      - It's an improper fraction.
      - All improper fractions can be transformed.
      - How many circles are colored in?
        - one
        - Four fourths is one and zero quarters.
  - Have your child divide the next circle into quarters.
    - Have them color in one quarter and write the total fraction under the circle. How much do they have colored in? They should write it as an improper fraction and as a mixed number. How many quarters are colored in? How many circles are colored in?
      - 5 quarters, 5/4
      - 1 ¼ circles
    - How do you get from the numbers 5/4 to 1 ¼? How are they related?
      - If you take four out of 5, you are left with one.
        - You can subtract, or if there were a lot of them, you could divide (which is just subtracting over and over again).
          - 5 divided by 4 is 1 with 1 left over. The remainder 1 goes over the four. There's one out of four parts remaining.
  - Have your child color in each of the remain quarters and tell you the improper fraction and mixed number each represents.
    - 6/4 and 1 2/4 or 1 ½
    - 7/4 and 1 ¾
    - 8/4 and 2
- Continued on the next page…

- Continue with the rest of the row, dividing the circles, coloring them in, and writing the mixed number and improper fraction for ¼ of the new circle.
  - The next will be 2 ¼ or 9/4.
    - You can take 4 out of 9 two times and one is left over. That one is one out of four parts.
    - Same way of saying…9 divided by 4 is 2, remainder 1.
    - The answer is written 2 ¼ .
- Your child can then continue on the worksheet from there.

Lesson 58

- Students will: add and subtract fractions and mixed numbers to solve word problems
- Ask your child how many cupcakes you would have eaten all together if you each had eaten one and a half.
  - 1 ½ + 1 ½ = 3 because 1 + 1 = 2 and ½ + ½ = 1   2 + 1 = 3
- When you add mixed numbers, you can split apart the whole numbers and add the whole numbers and fractions separately and then put them back together.
- Take a look at the Lesson 54 worksheet together. They will be doing more problems like this. They need to read the question carefully to figure out if they will be adding or subtracting. They can draw the picture in whatever way helps them solve the problem.
- Lesson 58 worksheet

Lesson 59

- Students will: solve word problems with mixed numbers
- Take a look at the example on the worksheet together.
  - Each line shows a quarter mile. Go line to line and count: ¼, ½, ¾, 1, 1 ¼ . Then count to see how far she walked: ¼, ½, ¾ is the answer.
  - Look at the subtraction problem. Add the answer to 1 ¼ to show that 2 − 1 ¼ = ¾
    - ¾ + 1 ¼ = 2 because and ¾ + ¼ = 1 and 1 + 1 = 2
    - ¾ + ¼ = $^4/_4$ When the numerator and denominator are the same, that's one whole. Think of a shape with all the parts colored in. Any fraction where the numerator and denominator are the same equals 1.
  - Look at the line chart again and count by half miles to two. Then draw in lines between each quarter marker and count to 2 miles by eighths.
    - $^1/_8$, $^2/_8$ (quarter line), $^3/_8$, $^4/_8$ (halfway), $^5/_8$, $^6/_8$, $^7/_8$, 1 mile…
- Lesson 59 worksheet
  - They need to use the diagrams and their brains to figure these out.

Lesson 60

- Students will: solve word problems with mixed numbers
- Lesson 60 worksheet
  - They can use the Lesson 59 worksheet page to help them if they need it.

Long Division

Lesson 61 (scissors, glue)

- Students will: learn long division
- Lesson 61 worksheets
  - There are a handful of pages for today.
    - First, cut out the line of terms on the first page.
    - Next, complete the worksheet page. They are using the example to write division problems in different ways.
    - Then, they are learning the terms.
      - The dividend, for the most part, is the biggest number. That's what you're dividing into parts.
      - The divisor is the number of parts you are dividing it into.
    - Finally, read through the three pages of an example problem.

Lesson 62 (scissors, glue)

- Students will: review the steps of long division
- Lesson 62 worksheet
  - Read through the example problem.
  - Cut and paste the steps. (Lesson 61+ worksheet has the pieces.)
  - Then your child should write out the steps. It would be great if they would not just write divide, multiply, etc. (though that would be okay), but would write complete sentences and use terms such as dividend and divisor.

Lesson 63

- Students will: understand multiplication and division are inverse operations
- Today's lesson is all about how division is the opposite of multiplication; that's what it means that they are inverse operations.
  - It's just like how addition and subtraction are opposites. You add three plus five and get eight and take eight and subtract five and get three.
  - Multiplication and division come in fact families as well, so to check your division answer, you can multiply the quotient by the divisor. The result should be the dividend.
- Lesson 63 worksheet
  - There are three different parts all dealing with multiplication and division as inverse operations.

Lesson 64 (scissors, glue)

- Students will: use long division
- They will need the numbers from the Lesson 61+ page for this.
- Lesson 64 worksheet
  - Solve the two problems.
    - They will place the numbers over each question mark.
    - After they have checked their answer, they can glue down the numbers.

Lesson 65

- Students will: practice long division
- Lesson 65 worksheet
  - These are long division problems with no remainders.
  - The bottom of the page are division word problems that just require knowing the facts.

Lesson 66 (an odd number of a few of things, different numbers 5 and up)

- Students will: find the remainder
- Have your child divide up the objects between the two of you. There should be one left over. That's the remainder.
  - Leave one of these set out when you look at the worksheet.
- Try it with all the objects and try it dividing one another way, like into three or four groups where it will have a remainder.
- Lesson 66 worksheet
  - Take a look at the top example. It shows how you can write the remainder as a fraction. When you were dividing the objects between yourselves, there was one of the two you needed at the end, one out of two.
  - It also shows how you can multiply and add to get back to the original number.
    - Use the objects you have divided between the both of you. Multiply and add to get back to the total number of objects.
      - You have two of them a certain number of times plus the one left over. That's what you are doing to get back to the original number. Gather them up as you multiply and add to get back to the total number.
  - In the word problems, there will be some left over. They should write the remainder as a fraction. The divisor is the denominator. In the first, the denominator will be six. In the second, it will be eight.

Lesson 67

- Students will: complete long division problems with remainders
- Lesson 67 worksheet
    - Look at the worksheet together. Look at the first one. Does four go into one?
        - No. They can write a zero there or a dash or just leave it blank. They will then check to see if four goes into thirteen.
        - They should write their remainders as fractions.

Lesson 68

- Students will: divide by double digits
- Go back to the Lesson 61 worksheet and talk through the steps of the double digit example.
- Lesson 68 worksheet
    - These are all double digit problems. This time they can write the remainder with an R.

Lesson 69

- Students will: divide by single and double digits into the thousands
- Lesson 69 worksheet
    - If they get any wrong, have them multiply their answer by the divisor to see if they get the dividend. Was it too high or too low?

Lesson 70

- Students will: divide by double digits
- Lesson 70 worksheet

Decimals

Lesson 71

- Students will: learn decimal point place value to the thousandths
- Look at this number with your child.

123456

    - Ask your child these questions and have them point to the answer.
    - Where would you put the decimal point to make the number say one and something?
        - after the one
    - Where would you put the decimal point to write the number twelve and something?
        - after the two

- o Where would you put the decimal point to write the number one hundred twenty-three and something?
    - ▪ after the three
- Draw a decimal point after the three in the long number.
    - o Ask your child to tell you what digit is in the tens, hundreds, and ones place.
        - ▪ tens, 2
        - ▪ hundreds, 1
        - ▪ ones, 3
    - o The digits after the decimal point have place values as well. There is no ones place after the decimal point. Each place over corresponds to the number of zeros. Let me explain with examples.
        - ▪ One decimal place is the tenths, and tens have one zero.
        - ▪ Two decimal places over is the hundredths, and hundreds have two zeros.
        - ▪ Three decimal places over is the thousandths, and thousands have three zeros.
    - o If you go back to the number example on the last page, the four is in the tenths place.
        - ▪ Ask your child what place value do the five and six have?
            - • hundredths, thousandths
    - o To move the decimal point back and forth you are just either multiplying or dividing by ten.
        - ▪ Try it with the example number. Make it bigger and smaller by moving the decimal point which is multiplying or dividing by ten.
- Lesson 71 worksheet

Lesson 72

- Students will: learn about the relationship between fractions, percent, and decimals; divide single digits into decimals
- Show this chart to your child and ask them to find the patterns.
    - o 100%   1.00 $100/100$
    - o 99%   0.99 $99/100$
    - o 90%   0.90 $90/100$
    - o 80%   0.80 $80/100$
    - o 75%   0.75 $75/100$
    - o 50%   0.50 $50/100$
    - o 25%   0.25 $25/100$
    - o 10%   0.10 $10/100$

- These are the same numbers again. What's different?
  - 100%   1   1
  - 99%   0.99 $99/100$
  - 90%   0.9 $9/10$
  - 80%   0.8 $4/5$
  - 75%   0.75 $3/4$
  - 50%   0.5 $1/2$
  - 25%   0.25 $1/4$
  - 10%   0.1 $1/10$
- It's easy to see the connection in the first set.
  - Percent is parts of one hundred.
  - The decimal are written with two digits going to the hundredths place, showing parts out of one hundred.
  - The fractions show how many out of one hundred.
  - They all show the same number.
- The second set is the same thing.
  - The percents are the same.
  - The decimals are the same but the final zeros are left off. They are not necessary to write. Think of a hundred's charts. If you colored in eight rows of ten on the chart, 80 out of the 100 blocks would be colored in.
    - 8 tenths is the same as 80 one hundredths.
  - The fractions are just reduced equivalent fractions. 50 out of 100 is half of them. Fifty hundredths equals one half.
- We'll be working on this throughout the week. They don't need to do anything with this today.
- On their worksheet they will continue to divide. There is a decimal point in the dividend. The only thing they need to do differently is put the decimal point in their answer directly above where it is in the dividend. That's like how when they add or subtract they bring the decimal point straight down.
- Lesson 72 worksheet
  - There are "regular" problems and word problems. They are all single digits dividing into a decimal.

Lesson 73

- Students will: convert fractions and decimals
- Look back at Lesson 72's percent, decimal, fraction chart. What was the pattern?
  - Then go to the worksheet to discuss today's lesson.
- Lesson 73 worksheet
  - At the top of the page, they will just need to place the digits in the decimals over ten, one hundred, or one thousand.
- Continued on the next page...

- o Remind your child that the number of digits after the decimal point relates to the number of zeros. One decimal place is tenths and tens have one zero, etc.
  - 0.1 = 1/10
- o The second part they will convert those fractions into equivalent fractions with ten and hundred in the denominator to easily find the decimal.
- o For the bottom section, they will have to divide to find the decimal.
  - Look at the example. These are all proper fractions, meaning they are all less than one.
  - The answers will all be decimals, numbers smaller than one.
  - The numerator becomes the dividend and the denominator becomes the divisor.
  - They will write a decimal point and any number of zeros after the dividend. 1 and 1.00000000 are the same number.
  - In the answer they will write the decimal point directly above. Each answer will begin 0.
- o Watch them work through the first of those problems to make sure they get how to set them up.

Lesson 74

- Students will: convert decimals and fractions
- Lesson 74 worksheet
  - o They can look back at the previous days if they need the reminder.
  - o They will use tens and hundreds to figure out decimals as well as dividing.
  - o They can use whatever is easiest for them.
    - If they can see that 50 is half of 100, then they just need to multiply 17 by 2 to find the decimal.
  - o They will find repeating decimals when they divide, 0.666… and 0.111…. You can point out, when they realize what's going on as they divide, that it will just repeat forever. There is no final answer. We write a line over the 6 or the 1 to show that it repeats.

Lesson 75

- Students will: convert fractions and decimals, add fractions with common denominators
- There are mixed numbers today. The whole number will stay the same whether a fraction or a decimal. Only the fractional part is changed into a decimal.
  - o Ask your child what decimal show one quarter.
    - 0.25 (like a quarter, 25 cents, $0.25)
    - How would they write five and a quarter as a fraction and as a decimal?
      - 5 ¼ and 5.25
- Lesson 75 worksheet

o At the bottom of the page, they will add and subtract fractions with common denominators. They only need to add and subtract the numerators. The denominators will stay the same.

Lesson 76

- Students will: add decimals
- Lesson 76 worksheet
  o Read through the directions together and use them to walk through the example on the page.
  o They will just be adding regularly. The important things is to make sure the place values are lining up. The decimal points need to be directly under each other, including the answer.

Lesson 77

- Students will: subtract decimals
- Lesson 77 worksheet
  o Read through the directions together and use them to walk through the example on the page.
  o They will just be subtracting regularly. Just like Lesson 76, the important things are to make sure the place values are lining up. The decimal points need to be directly under each other, including the answer.

Lesson 78

- Students will: multiply decimals
- Lesson 78 worksheet
  o As the other days, read the directions and see the steps in the example.
  o Underline the 0, 3, and 1 in the decimal places. Count them: 1, 2, 3. Underline each digit in the answer that's in a decimal place. There are three. There will always be the same number of decimal places in the answer as in the problem.
    ▪ If there is a zero at the end of the decimal, that can be left off the final answer.

Lesson 79

- Students will: multiply decimals with one decimal place, identify place value to the thousands and thousandths
- Lesson 79 worksheet (Look at this together.)
  o They will just multiply normally and then get the decimal point in the correct place in the answer.
  o You can ask your child how many decimal places each answer will have.
    ▪ 2
    ▪ If the last digit is a zero, that should be left off.
  o Have your child name the place value of each box in part B.
    ▪ thousands, hundreds, tens, ones, tenths, hundredths, thousandths

Lesson 80

- Students will: multiply decimals with two decimal places
- Lesson 80 worksheet
  - You can ask your child how many decimal places will be in each answer.
    - 4

Lesson 81

- Students will: add and subtract decimals
- Ask your child how to add and subtract decimals.
  - They will add and subtract normally. They just need make sure to keep all of their place values lined up and to drop the decimal point straight down into the answer.
- Lesson 81 worksheet
  - There is addition and subtraction, so they will need to pay attention to the sign.
  - Part B has magic squares. They just need to start with the row or column with two numbers, fill in the blank, and then continue in the same way.

Lesson 82 (coins and ones, have at least 4 pennies, 2 dimes, 1 nickel, 3 quarters)

- Students will: make change
- Practice making change. Instead of subtracting, they can count onto the cost amount until they get to the amount paid. That's the change.
  - For instance, have your child use the coins and bills to make change for $18.79 when you paid $20.00.
    - They should start with the smallest amount.
      - They can put down a penny to make 80.
      - Then they can put down two dimes to make $19.
      - Then one dollar to make 20.
      - Have them add up and announce the change, $1.21.
  - Have your child try again with making change for $18.37 when you paid $20.00.
    - They can put down three pennies to make 40. (They can count: 38, 39, 40 as they put each down.)
    - They can put a dime down to make 50.
    - They can put two quarters down to make $19.
      - They could do that many ways, but the goal is to use as few coins as possible.
    - Then one dollar to make 20.
      - The change total is $1.63.

- Lesson 82 worksheet
  - You can ask your child how many decimal places will be in each answer.
    - 2
  - They will write how many of each coin they will give as change, trying to use as few as possible. They will also write the change total. They can use the coins to help them

Lesson 83 (coins and bills, have at least 4 pennies, 2 dimes, 1 nickel, 3 quarters)

- Students will: make change, subtract from $100.00
- Have your child write down any money amount under $100 including decimals with no zeros in the number.
  - Have your child subtract that amount from $100.00.
    - They just need to draw a box around 100.0 and take away one, making it 99.9. The final zero becomes ten.
      - This is just borrowing, but instead of borrowing one at a time, you are taking one away from the whole number at once. One less than 1000 is 999.
    - Then they can just subtract straight down.
- They will also be making change with some bigger differences today, but I don't think they need the extra practice unless you had fun making change together. If you want to practice, work on making change to ten and one hundred dollars.
- Lesson 83 worksheet

Lesson 84

- Students will: divide with decimals
- Take a look at the example problem on their worksheet.
- Lesson 84 worksheet
  - Read through the directions on the page and use them to look at the example problem. Talk about the examples below before they begin to work.
  - They will just ignore the decimal point, divide as normal, and then put the decimal point directly above the dividend in the answer.
  - However, there is an extra step if there is a decimal point in the divisor.
    - They have to get rid of it by moving the decimal point over. However many places the decimal point moves in the divisor, it moves in the dividend.

$$.24 \div .4 = 2.4 \div 4 = .6$$

$$1.21 \div .11 = 121 \div 11 = 11$$

$$10.24 \div .16 = 1024 \div 16 = 64$$

No decimal places

Lesson 85

- Students will: write division problems in different ways including fractions
- Look at the example below. They all say 12 divided by 3.

$$12 \div 3 = 3\overline{)12} = {}^{12}\!/_3$$

- A fraction tells us what part of something it is. That's just like dividing. When we divide, we divide something into sections. Three is in the denominator. There are three parts. When you divide twelve into three parts, you get four. You wouldn't write twelve thirds as your answer. You would reduce and simplify and write 4 as the answer.
- Lesson 85 worksheet
  - They need to fill in all the blanks. You could check their first one to make sure they are getting the numbers in the correct places, and then they can refer to that one to complete the rest.

Lesson 86

- Students will: convert fractions into decimals, compare decimals
- Lesson 86 worksheet
  - They will divide the fractions to find their decimal equivalent.
  - Important! They only need to divide it enough to figure out which is greater. Some of those decimals go on and on.
  - Then they will compare the fractions. You can ask your child to make sure they remember which way to point the greater than/less than symbol.
  - There's an example on the page.

Lesson 87

- Students will: multiply three digits by three digits
- Lesson 87 worksheet
  - They have to complete five. Check their work. If they get one wrong, then they have to do another one. If they get two wrong, they have to do two more, etc. Please require this even if they make even a little mistake.
  - You could also offer a reward to a child who doesn't have to but completes the page anyway.

Lesson 88

- Students will: divide two digits into four digits
- Look at an example together. You can write out the steps as you go.

$$32\overline{)1440}$$

  - 32 doesn't go into 1 or 14, so they can start with 144.

- o 32 goes into 144 <u>four</u> times. How do I know?
  - ▪ 30 x 5 is 150 and 30 x 4 is 120
- o 32 x 4 = 120 + 8 = 128
- o 144 – 128 = 16
- o 32 goes into 160 <u>five</u> times because…
  - ▪ 30 x 5 = 150 and 30 x 6 = 180
- o 32 x 5 = 150 + 10 = 160
- o 45
- Lesson 88 worksheet
  - o This will work like Lesson 87, having to do more if they made a mistake. This is to encourage paying attention and not making sloppy mistakes.

Lesson 89

- Students will: add fractions with common denominators, simplify fractions by finding equivalent fractions
- Ask your child to reduce five tenths. What fraction with a lower denominator could you write it as?
  - o If the numerator can be divided into the denominator, divide both by the number.
  - o $5 \div 5 = 1$ and $10 \div 5 = 2$
  - o Five tenths can be **reduced** or **simplified** to one half.
- Ask your child to reduce six tenths.
  - o If the top and bottom number are even, you know you can at divide the top and bottom both by two.
  - o $6 \div 2 = 3$ and $10 \div 2 = 5$
  - o Six tenths reduces to three fifths.
- Ask your child to reduce six ninths.
  - o They aren't both even and the numerator doesn't divide into the denominator. These are the hardest.
    - ▪ They can see that you can divide three into both.
  - o $6 \div 3 = 2$ and $9 \div 3 = 3$
  - o Six ninths reduces to two thirds.
- Lesson 89 worksheet
  - o They will add and reduce the fractions as much as possible.

Lesson 90

- Students will: convert fractions to decimals, add mixed numbers
- Lesson 90 worksheet
  - o For the first part, tell your child those are decimal and fraction counterparts that are good ones to just know and recognize.

Lesson 91

- Students will: multiply fractions, reduce and simplify fractions, complete mental math operations, practice speed in answering addition facts
- Lesson 91+ worksheet
  - Read the questions to your child and have them write the answers only on the page.
  - Read them each once only. You can reread them as you go back over it to check the answers.
    - Start with 8, add 3, add 5, add 2, add 4. **22**
    - 653 minus 100. **553**
    - What is 191 plus 10? **201**
    - How many inches in one foot? **12 inches**
    - What is 8 hundreds and seven ones? **807**
    - What is 54 minus 40? **14**
    - About how much is 531 minus 261? **530 – 260 = 270 or 500-300**
    - Brett left at 3 and came back at 4. How long was he gone? **1 hour**
- Lesson 91 facts page
  - Set a timer for three minutes for your child to try to finish the page. You can decide if you want to offer a reward.
- They will be multiplying fractions today.
- To multiply fractions you just multiply the numerators together and multiply the denominators together.
  - Let me talk about why for a moment. Fractions work differently.
  - One half times one half is not one half two times as in one half plus one half. That would be one half times two.
  - One half plus one half equals 1 but one half times one half equals one quarter.
  - What we're really saying is one half OF one half when we are multiplying fractions. OF is a clue to multiply things together.
  - If you divide a square in half and then divide half of that in half, you end up with one quarter. That's what we're doing when we're multiplying.
  - When you multiply a fraction by a whole number, you still multiply the numerators together and the denominators together.
    - When you multiply a whole number by a fraction, the whole number is the numerator. It has an invisible one as a denominator.
    - Remember fractions are just division problems. Whole numbers are division problems with that number over one. Any number divided by one is just itself. The whole number is the simplified version of the fraction.
    - When you multiply a fraction by whole number, the whole number acts as the numerator and is multiplied by the numerator.
    - The denominator stays the same because it's just being multiplied by one.

- Lesson 91 worksheet
    - Read through the directions at the top of the page together.
    - Ask your child what clues to look for to help them reduce and simplify the fraction answers.
        - Two even numbers can each be divided by two.
        - Check to see if the denominator can be divided by the numerator. If so, divide them both by the numerator and the numerator will become one.
        - See if any number divides into both the numerator and the denominator. (For instance, if they both end in either a 5 or a 0, then they can both be divided by 5.)

Lesson 92

- Students will: multiply fractions, reduce and simplify fractions, divide one digit into hundreds, complete mental math operations, practice speed in answering multiplication facts
- Lesson 91+ worksheet
    - Read the questions to your child and have them write the answers only on the page.
        - $55 + 6 =$ **61**
        - $89 - 50 =$ **39**
        - About how much $250 + 301$? **$250 + 300 = 550$**
        - What is $77 + 30$? **107 (notice $70 + 30 = 100$)**
        - How many 2s in 18? **9 (9x2=18)**
        - What number is 3 thousands and 9 tens and 1 one? **3091**
        - What is 5×10? **50**
        - How many hours are in a day? **24 hours**
- Lesson 92 facts page
    - Set a timer for three minutes for your child to try to finish the page. You can decide if you want to offer a reward.
- Lesson 92 worksheet
    - Your child might like to know a trick to make multiplying and reducing these fractions easier.
    - Look at the first one. You can write next to it 1 x 4, as the numerator, over 2 x 7, as the denominator. Do you see how it's a fraction? That's a division problem. You can divide and simplify even before you begin. That will make the numbers smaller for multiplying and maybe you won't have to reduce the fractions at all at the end because you've already basically reduced the fraction.
        - You have two even numbers, so you can divide them both by two.
        - Cross off the two and write a 1. Cross off the four and write a 2.
        - Now multiply: 1 x 2 = 2 and 1 x 7 = 7

o Go through the rest of the fractions together. You don't have to write out that extra step. Just cross out the numbers right where they are in the fractions. It has to be one in the numerator and one in the denominator, and they have to be divided by the same number.

- Going down the column on the left, you can divide the 2 and 4, the 2 and 6, and the 2 and 8 each by two.
- Going down the right column: you can divide the 2 and 6 by 2, the 3 and 9 by 3, the 3 and 12 by 3, and the 5 and 15 by 5.

o This is what you would be doing when you reduce a fraction at the end, but this makes it easier because you are working with smaller numbers.

o Now your child can multiply and probably won't have to reduce anything.

o There are also long division problems on the page. Your child can turn back to Lessons 61-65 for a reminder of the division steps.

Lesson 93

- Students will: divide fractions, reduce and simplify fractions, complete mental math operations, practice speed in answering subtraction facts
- Lesson 91+ worksheet
  o Read the questions to your child and have them write the answers only on the page.
  - How much greater is 100 than 80? **20**
  - Round 463 to the nearest 100. **500**
  - Start with 6, add 9, add 5, subtract 4. **16**
  - How much is 9 tens? **90**
  - Tom weighs 70 lbs. Shawn is 12 lbs. heavier. How much does Shawn weigh? **82 lbs.**
  - Write the next three numbers: 12, 14, 16, … **18, 20, 22**
  - What number is 20 less than 90? **70**
  - Estimate $947 - 211$. **$950 - 210 = 740$ or $900 - 200 = 700$**
- Lesson 93 facts page
  o Set a timer for three minutes for your child to try to finish the page. You can decide if you want to offer a reward.
- Ask your child what the reciprocal of a fraction is.
  o That's the upside version of it. The denominator becomes the numerator and the numerator becomes the denominator.
- We saw that when you multiply a fraction by a proper fraction it gets smaller. ½ x ½ is ¼, a smaller amount.
- Division is the opposite of multiplication. Ask what's going to happen when you divide by a proper fraction.
  o The answer is going to get bigger.
- Lesson 93 worksheet
  o Read the directions together.
  o Watch your child do the first one. The first step should be to write it as a multiplication problem with the second number as its reciprocal.
  o Then they can simplify before they multiply if they think that's easier.
  o There's not a lot of room, so they need to write neatly.

Lesson 94

- Students will: divide single digits into hundreds, complete mental math operations, practice speed in answering division facts
- Lesson 91+ worksheet
    - Read the questions to your child and have them write the answers only on the page.
        - Round 26 to the nearest 10. **30**
        - What time is 20 minutes before 6:40? **6:20**
        - Write the next three numbers: 15, 13, 11, … **9, 7, 5**
        - How much is 4 x 100? **400**
        - How much greater is 110 than 100? **10**
        - Estimate 672 – 499. **670 – 500 = 170 or 700 – 500 = 200**
        - Write the number that is 4 tens and 2 ones. **42**
        - Write the number that is 3 tens and 6 ones. **36**
- Lesson 94 facts page
    - Set a timer for three minutes for your child to try to finish the page. You can decide if you want to offer a reward.
- Lesson 94 worksheet
    - They should write their remainders as fractions. Do they remember how?

Lesson 95

- Students will: divide whole numbers and fractions
- Lesson 95 worksheet
    - Have your child show you how they would attempt the first one.
        - They need to put the whole number over one.
        - They need to rewrite it as a multiplication problem with the reciprocal of the second number.
        - They can then simplify and multiply or multiply and then simplify.
    - When they are figuring out the puzzle, the easiest thing to do would be to cross off each answer it couldn't be according to the clues and then see what's left.

Averages

Lesson 96

- Students will: learn about averages including finding the range, mode, median, and mean of a set of numbers
- There are several ways we find averages, the descriptive amount of what's normal for a set of numbers.
- Ask your child how they would find the average height of a group of kids if they didn't have anything to measure them with?
    - They could line them up and see what's the middle height.
    - They could see what height is the most common.

- The **median** is the middle number. You line up all your data, all your numbers (or all your kids) and choose the one in the middle.
  - The only tricky part is if there is an even number. In that case, find what's in the middle of the middle. Here are two examples.
    - 1 2 3 4 5 6
      - Where's the middle of this list of numbers?
        - between 3 and 4
        - What's in the middle of 3 and 4?
          - 3 ½ or 3.5
    - 2 4 6 8
      - Where's the middle of this list of numbers?
        - between 4 and 6
        - What's in the middle of 4 and 6?
          - 5
- The **mode** is the number that's there the most.
  - What's the mode of this list of numbers?
    - 3, 6, 7, 5, 4, 5, 5, 6
      - There are more fives than any other number.
- The **range** is the difference between the lowest and highest numbers. What is the range of the last list of numbers?
  - $7 - 3 = 4$
- Finally, the **mean** is how we find the average mathematically.
  - You add up all the numbers and then divide by how many numbers there are.
  - What's the mean of the list of even numbers above?
    - Add them up.
      - $2 + 4 + 6 + 8 = 20$
    - There are four numbers in the list.
      - 20 divided by 4 is 5.
    - The mean is 5.
- Lesson 96 worksheet
  - The definitions of these terms are on the page as a reminder.

Lesson 97

- Students will: find the mean, mode, range, and median of sets of numbers
- Lesson 97 worksheet
  - They can look back at Lesson 96 if they need a reminder.

Lesson 98

- Students will: divide fractions; find the mean, mode, median, and range of a set of numbers
- Lesson 98 worksheet
    - Ask your child to tell you the range of the set of numbers.
        - 11 to 84, 84 – 11 = 73

Lesson 99

- Students will: find the mean, median, mode, and range of sets of numbers
- Ask your child what the total is of a set of numbers if the mean of five numbers is 8. How would they know?
    - We know that the total divided by five is eight.
    - 8 x 5 = 40   Forty divided by five is eight.
    - There are puzzles like that on their worksheet today.
- Lesson 99 worksheet
    - They can use mental math to add up the numbers in the lists.

Lesson 100

- Students will: make change, round to the nearest ten, hundred, thousand
- Lesson 100 worksheet
    - Ask your child to name the place values of the digits in the last number in the rounding section.
        - 2, ones
        - 6, tens
        - 1, hundreds
        - 4, thousands
        - 3, ten thousands
    - Ask your child to round that to the nearest ten thousand.
        - They would look at the number to its right, the 4 in the thousands place. It's less than five so it rounds down to 30,000.

Percent

Lesson 101

- Students will: be introduced to percent
- Lesson 101 worksheet
  - Look at the definition together. A percent is just a way to write a fraction out of 100.
    - How would they write the fraction that represents the first picture there?
      - Five are colored in, so five over one hundred.
      - That's five percent. That's all percent is, an expressions of a fraction of one hundred.
    - How would they write six tenths as a percent?
      - Six tenths equals sixty hundredths, 60%.
  - To find a percent of something, you multiply. The word OF is a clue to multiply.
    - 25% of 20 is $^{25}/_{100}$ times 20.

Lesson 102

- Students will: convert between decimals, fractions, and percents
- They have also already worked on converting fractions and decimals. Ask your child how to convert these into a fractions.

$$0.6 \qquad 0.35$$

  - Just have them read the decimals out loud.
    - six tenths
    - thirty-five hundredths
    - That tells you the fractions right there.
      - The six is one decimal place, so that is tenths because ten has one zero. It is written 6 over 10.
        - Then you reduce. Six and ten are both even, so you can divide both by two.
          - The answer is three fifths.
      - Thirty-five is written over one hundred. (Two decimal places is hundredths, and hundred has two zeros.)
        - Then you reduce. The numerator and denominator both end in either a five or a zero, so we know we can divide both by five.
          - The answer is seven twentieths.
  - Ask your child how to convert those fractions back into a decimal?
    - You divide.
    - The denominator is divided into the numerator.

- o Now how do you change those decimals into a percent?
  - ▪ A percent is a hundredth, out of one hundred. To make a percent out of a decimal, you take the hundredth out of the decimal, meaning, you move the decimal point to after the hundredth place.
    - • Put your pencil point on the decimal point and then jump it two places to the right so that the hundredth is no longer part of the decimal.
    - • 0.35 becomes 35%. They both say 35 out of 100.
    - • 0.6 becomes 60%. Remember there are an infinite amount of invisible zeros after a decimal point.
  - o Ask your child what 0.358 would be as a percent? (Write an 8 at the end of the decimal above.)
    - ▪ They just need to move the decimal point two places (to the same point as before).
    - ▪ The answer is 35.8%.
  - o Lesson 102 worksheet
    - ▪ They will be converting between decimals, fractions, and percent. They need to find the decimal and then they can easily change that into a percent.

Lesson 103

- • Students will: convert between fractions, decimals, percents
- • Lesson 103 worksheet
  - o You can ask your child if they want to talk through the different conversions again from Lesson 102. They can also use their Lesson 102 page for a reminder of how to do it.

Lesson 104

- • Students will: convert between fractions, decimals, percents
- • Lesson 104 worksheet
  - o They can use the previous two lessons as a reminder.

Lesson 105

- • Students will: convert between decimals, fractions, percents
- • Ask your child how to write three and a half as a decimal and a fraction.
  - o 3 ½ and 3.5
  - o They will have some mixed numbers on today's worksheet. They should realize that the whole number doesn't change at all from the fraction to the decimal. Only the fractional part will change.
  - o What's 3.5 as a percent?
    - ▪ 350%, just move the decimal point over, but it's going to be over one hundred percent because of the whole number.

- Ask your child to write the number twelve and one hundred thirty-two thousandths.
  - 12.132
  - Ask your child to name each decimal place.
    - tens, ones, tenths, hundredths, thousandths (One thousand has 3 zeros.)
  - Ask your child how to write 2 and 5 thousandths.
    - 2.005
      - The five needs to go in the thousandths place.
- Lesson 105 worksheet
  - They will be doing each of these things.

Word Problems

Lesson 106

- Students will: use percents to solve word problems
- Try some together before they begin.
  - If you bought something for $20.00 and paid 6% tax, how much did you have to pay?
    - Ask your child how they would figure it out.
    - They need to find 6% of 20 and then add that amount onto the $20 price.
      - To find 6% they multiply by six hundredths. They could use a fraction or a decimal, but since we're dealing with money, a decimal is probably best.
        - 0.06 x 20 = 1.20
        - 1.20 + 20 = $21.20
  - If there was a 15% sale on an item that was $30, how much does it cost?
    - Ask your child to tell you how to solve it.
      - This time you will subtract.
        - 0.15 x 30 = 4.50
        - 30 – 4.50 = $25.50
- Lesson 106 worksheet
  - It's all word problems of this sort. They need to pay attention to what the question is asking.

Lesson 107

- Students will: solve story problems
- Lesson 107 worksheet
  - They need to pay attention to the question. Not all information will be used every time.

Lesson 108

- Students will: solve story problems
- Lesson 108 worksheet
  - They should pay attention to the question. Not all information will be used every time.

Lesson 109

- Students will: solve story problems
- Lesson 109 worksheet
  - They should pay attention to the question. Not all information will be used every time.

Lesson 110

- Students will: solve story problems
- Lesson 110 worksheet
  - They should pay attention to the question. Not all information will be used every time.

Rounding Decimals

Lesson 111

- Students will: round decimals to the nearest whole number, tenth, and hundredth; identify place value to the ten thousandth
- Ask your child to read this number.

123,456.789

  - It's one hundred twenty-three thousand, four hundred fifty-six AND seven hundred eighty-nine thousandths.
    - Go through each digit and name the place value.
      - 1 – hundred thousands
      - 2 – ten thousands
      - 3 – thousands
      - 4 – hundreds
      - 5 – tens
      - 6 – ones
      - 7 – tenths
      - 8 – hundredths
      - 9 – thousandths

- If there were another digit on the end, what would be its place value?
  - ten thousandths (four decimal places, four zeros in ten thousand)
- Now round the number to each place value.
  - hundred thousands – 100,000
  - ten thousands – 120,000
  - thousands – 123,000
  - hundreds – 123,500
  - tens – 123,460
  - ones – 123,457
  - tenths – 123,456.8
  - hundredths – 123,456.79
- What is our number multiplied by ten?
  - Zeros and decimal places are related. To change the number one into a ten, we add a zero. The zero changes the place value. Moving the decimal point also changes the place value. That's what adding a zero when we multiply by ten or two zeros when we multiply by one hundred does, move the decimal point over, changing the place value.
    - 1,234,567.89
      - Can your child read the number?
        - one million, two hundred thirty-four thousand, five hundred sixty-seven AND eighty-nine hundredths
- What is our number multiplied by 100?
  - The decimal point needs to move two times.
  - Have your child read the number.
    - 12,345,678.9
      - twelve million, three hundred forty-five thousand, six hundred seventy-eight AND nine tenths
- This week they will be identifying place value in decimals and rounding decimals. Everything to the left of the place value that they are rounding to is going to stay the same.
- Lesson 111 worksheet

Lesson 112

- Students will: identify place value of decimals, multiply
- Lesson 112 worksheet
  - They will write out the numbers and find the place value of digits.
  - The final section is to keep up with what they know.

Lesson 113

- Students will: round decimals, divide
- Lesson 113 worksheet
  - They will round the decimals according to the directions. They need to pay attention to which place they are working with.
  - The final section is to keep up with what they know.

Lesson 114

- Students will: add decimals, round decimals
- Lesson 114 worksheet
  - They will add the decimals. They can use the spaces around the boxes as scratch pad. They add just like regular numbers. The important thing is to add the same place values together. Tenths get added to tenths, etc.

Lesson 115

- Students will: identify decimals on a number line
- Lesson 115 worksheet
  - Take a look at it together.
  - Each line is a tenth of the first number shown.
    - That means on the first number line each line is one tenth, 0.1.
    - On the second number line each line is one hundredth, 0.01.
    - On the third number line each line is one thousandth, 0.001.
  - Have your child say the numbers along the number lines until comfortable.
    - The first one after the middle number on each line is: 1.1, 0.11, 0.011

Time

Lesson 116

- Students will: draw hands on clocks to the nearest minutes, find the missing operation, practice quickly solving arithmetic problems
- Lesson 116 worksheet
  - You don't need to review time unless your child needs you to.
  - For the second section they just need to think. If they think they don't know, they just need to try each operation in the blank until one works.
  - For the last section, you could time them and encourage them to move quickly, as long as they are accurate! To find the average, just take the total number of seconds (2 minutes = 120 seconds) and divide by the total number of problems, 11.

Lesson 117

- Students will: draw hands on clocks, identify times, determine elapsed time, solve word problems
- Lesson 117 worksheet
  - For the elapsed time problems, point out to your child that they should first count on the minutes and then count on the hours because the minutes may move the time to the next hour. They can use the lines on the clocks to jump along to count.

Lesson 118

- Students will: determine elapsed time, solve word problems
- Lesson 118 worksheet
  - They can turn back to the clocks on the previous page if they want something visual to count around to determine the elapsed time. I do recommend counting on the minutes and then the hours.

Geometry

Lesson 119

- Students will: solve word problems, learn about 2D shapes
- Lesson 119 worksheet
  - You could quiz your child on some of the shapes by having them draw them.

Lesson 120 (scissors, glue)

- Students will: learn about one, two, and three dimensions as well as 3D shapes and how nets transform into 3-D shapes
- Introduce dimensions

This is a line. It has one dimension.
All one dimensional shapes only have length.
The only 1D shape is a line, whether straight or wavy.

This is a rectangle. It has two dimensions: length and width. All 2D shapes have an area but no depth. Some 2D shapes are triangles, rectangles, pentagons, etc.

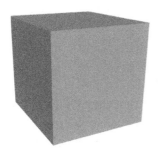

This is a cube. It has three dimensions: length, width, and depth. All 3D shapes are solids.

- Have your child look over the shapes and the nets. A net is a 3D shape opened up. They could cut out and build the dodecahedron on the second page. Save this for Lesson 122 if you make it.
- Lesson 120 worksheet
  - There are word problems and nets to try to figure out.

Lesson 121

- Students will: identify 3D shapes, solve word problems
- You can check to see if your child remembers how to find the average.
  - They find the total and then divide by how many numbers there are.
  - You can have them find the average of 1, 2, 3, 4, 5.
    - total 15, number 5
    - average 3
- You can also check their memory on percent. How do you find 15% of $10?
  - Convert the percent to a decimal and multiply.
  - Multiply 10 by 0.15. = $1.50
- Lesson 121 worksheet
  - They will match the shapes and answer the questions in the word problems.

Lesson 122 (your dodecahedron or a box/cube/block, optional: coins)

- Students will: identify edges, faces, and vertices of a shape; use the least number of coins, identify a shape from its net
- Get out the dodecahedron if you made it or grab a block or die or box.
  - Each flat surface is a **face**. They must be flat to be a face.
  - Each edge is an **edge**. That's the line between two faces.
  - All the points, the corners, are called **vertices**. One point, one corner is called a **vertex**, but you won't find a closed shape with just one.
    - Edges connect vertices. If there are no vertices, there are no edges.
- Have your child count them up on the dodecahedron or a box/block.
  - A dodecahedron has 30 edges, 12 faces, and 20 vertices.
  - A box has 6 faces, 8 vertices, and 12 edges.
- Ask your child how many would a sphere have?
  - none
- What about a cylinder?
  - no vertices, no edges, two faces (the top and bottom circles)

- Lesson 122 worksheet
  - For the coin section, they need to pay attention to use the least number of coins. You could give them a pile of coins to work with if that helps.

Lesson 123 (piece of paper)

- Students will: identify lines of symmetry
- A **line of symmetry** is where a shape can be divided in half perfectly. If you folded the shape over that line, the two sides would perfectly line up. It's not just dividing the amount of space in half, it's having two exactly equal and opposite sides.
- Have your child take a piece of paper and find the lines of symmetry.
  - There are two: down the middle top to bottom and right to left.
  - Along the diagonals are not lines of symmetry. They can fold it along those lines to see the two sides don't match up.
- A unique shape is the circle. It has an infinite number of lines of symmetry. You can draw a line across from any point on the circle to the point directly across from it and it would be a line of symmetry. If you could draw small enough, you could draw an infinite number of lines of symmetry.
- Lesson 123 worksheet
  - They can use the images to draw lines of symmetry. They need to always be thinking about folding along those lines and having the two sides match up.

Lesson 124 (three pencils or pens)

- Students will: learn about angles
- Take a look at the Lesson <u>125</u> worksheet.
  - Those are protractors. They measure angles. An **angle** is how we measure a turn.
  - Put two pencils together and rotate one, keeping them touching at one end.
    - The angle is measured in degrees. We write the angle at the point where two lines touch and use the degree symbol which is a little circle. You can see an example just below.
    - Here's what we call a **right angle**. It measures 90 degrees.

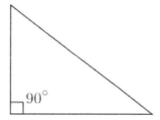

  - Using two pencils, ask your child to make a 90 degree angle.
  - Have your child close the pencils some to a smaller angle.

- Go back to the worksheet. Any angle that is smaller than 90 degrees is an **acute angle** because everything little is cute!
  - Find acute angles on the page.
  - A straight line is 180 degrees. Have your child make 180 degrees with the pencils.
  - Any angle between 90 and 180 is an **obtuse angle**. Find some obtuse angles on the page.
  - A **reflex angle** is one that's bigger than 180. Have your child make a reflex angle with the pencils.
    - They can see that a reflex angle measured another way is an acute or obtuse angle.
  - Have your child lay the three pencils in a straight line. Ask your child how many degrees is a straight line.
    - 180 degrees (Any point to any other point is a turn of 180 degrees.)
    - Have your child make a triangle with the three pencils.
      - The measure of the three angles inside of a triangle is always 180 degrees.
    - Have them open and close the triangle again and watch the angles.
  - Any circle or around any point is 360 degrees.
    - Have your child trace a circle with their finger from a point on a pencil up and around and across and under the pencil and back to the point.
    - The circle went 180 degrees on the top of the pencil and then 180 degrees under the pencil.
- Lesson 124 worksheet
  - They need these vocabulary words to answer the questions.
  - They also need to know which way is clockwise, the way the hands move around the clock.

Lesson 125

- Students will: measure angles using protractors
- Lesson 125 worksheet
  - Look at the worksheet together. They will read the measure of the angles. When it starts on 0, they can just read the second number. That's the angle. When it doesn't start on zero, they need to find the difference between the angles. They can subtract or just use their finger and jump and count along the protractor to find the angle.
  - They need to write the angle measurements with a degree symbol!

Lesson 126

- Students will: label angles, identify angle types
- Review with your child the degrees for the following types of angles: straight, right, reflex, obtuse, acute. They are all defined for you on Lesson 124 in this book.
- Lesson 126 worksheet
  - Look at the example together. That's how to label an angle.
    - The name of the angle is labeled with the angle symbol and then a letter. It can also be labeled by telling three points: two points on the lines and the vertex point in the middle.
  - They should use the example to do the others.
  - They can look back at previous pages to help with parts B and C.

Lesson 127

- Students will: convert between metric measurements
- Take a look at the chart on the Lesson 127 worksheet together. Ask your child these example questions.
  - How many centimeters is 2 meters?
    - 200 centimeters
    - You multiply by 100 to get from meters to centimeters.
  - How many meters is 500 centimeters?
    - 5 meters
    - You divide by 100 to get from centimeters to meters.
      - That's the same as moving the decimal place to the left two places.
      - What would be 50 centimeters in meters?
        - 0.5 meters
  - What is 1.5 liters in milliliters?
    - 1500 ml
    - You multiply by 1000, which is moving the decimal point three places to the right.
  - What's 2800 milliliters in liters?
    - 2.8 L
    - They divide by 1000 or move the decimal point three places to the left.
  - They should use the chart to check to make sure their answer makes sense. They should check which number is supposed to be bigger.
- Lesson 127 worksheet
  - They will be converting between measurements at the top of the page and in the word problems.

Lesson 128

- Students will: read rulers to the tenth and sixteenth, find the perimeter
- Ask your child if they know how to find the perimeter.
  - It's the measure around a shape.
  - They can add each side, or if sides have the same length, like a square or regular octagon or hexagon and such, they can use multiplication.
  - How would they find the perimeter of a square with a side length of 5?
    - 5 x 4 = 20
  - How would they find the perimeter of a rectangle with a length of 5 and width of 3?
    - 5 x 2 = 10 (the two long sides)
    - 3 x 2 = 6 (the two short sides)
    - 10 + 6 = 16 perimeter
- Lesson 128 worksheet
  - Take a look at the worksheet page together.
  - Look at the rulers and have your child count a little ways on each to show they can read it.
    - On the centimeter ruler each line is a tenth.
      - one tenth, two tenths, ….two and one tenth, two and two tenths
    - On the inch ruler each line is a sixteenth. Do the same thing.
      - The middle line is eight sixteenths.

Lesson 129 (ruler, piece of paper)

- Students will: find the perimeter and the area
- The area of a shape is the measure of the space inside of it.
  - Have your child use a ruler to draw a box that is four centimeters by three centimeters.
    - Then have your child draw boxes inside of it. Each box will be one centimeter wide and one centimeter high. There will be four boxes across and three boxes high.
    - Each box is a square centimeter.
      - That's how you measure area. The square of a measure.
        - When we measure perimeter, one would be one line segment.
        - When we measure area, one centimeter means one whole box.
  - To find area of a shape like a square and a rectangle, we multiply the length times the width. On a square, those are the same number.
    - What would be the area of a square with a side of 5 cm?
      - 25 centimeters squared
      - We write 25 cm^2.

- What would be the area of a rectangle with sides of 4 inches and 8 inches?
    - 32 in^2
- Lesson 129 worksheet
    - They will have to find perimeter and area.
    - On the bottom ones they will have to figure it out.
        - The trick is to draw a line on each to turn them into two rectangles. Then they can add the two areas together.

Lesson 130

- Students will: find the missing number in area problems, convert between measurements
- Lesson 131 worksheet
    - They just need to use their brains on this. They can try different numbers if they aren't sure. (They really need to divide to find the answer to the top questions, as dividing is the opposite of multiplying, but they can just try a number in the missing spot and see if it's right or too high or low and work from there.)
    - For the bottom of the page, they need to use the chart given. They are all equal. What would be 2 gallons in each measure?
        - 8 quarts, 16 pints, 32 cups, etc.

Review

Lesson 131

- Students will: perform addition operations for speed and accuracy, add multiple addends
- You could time the first set of problems on the page and have them record their time at the top. They could try to beat their time each day.
    - You could consider a reward for beating their time and a reward for not making any mistakes on the bottom section.
- Lesson 131 worksheet
    - This is review but the bottom problems will have to take some careful work. They could split them and add two at a time and then combine them.

Lesson 132

- Students will: perform subtraction operations for speed and accuracy, subtract four-digit numbers
- You could time the first set of problems on the page and have them record their time at the top. They could try to beat their time each day.
    - You could consider a reward for beating their time and a reward for not making any mistakes on the bottom section.
- Lesson 132 worksheet
    - They just need to work carefully.

Lesson 133
- Students will: perform multiplication operations for speed and accuracy, multiply four-digit numbers
- You could time the first set of problems on the page and have them record their time at the top. They could try to beat their time each day.
  - You could consider a reward for beating their time and a reward for not making any mistakes on the bottom section.
- Lesson 133 worksheet
  - They need to write carefully and make sure they line up all their place values correctly. They just multiply each place value one at a time and write it in the correct column.

Lesson 134

- Students will: perform division operations for speed and accuracy, divide two digits into four digits
- You could time the first set of problems on the page and have them record their time at the top. They could try to beat their time each day.
  - You could consider a reward for beating their time and a reward for not making any mistakes on the bottom section.
- Lesson 134 worksheet

Lesson 135

- Students will: find elapsed time, convert 24-hour time, convert time measurements
- There is one thing that's new on this worksheet, 24 hour time. In Europe and Asia, time is given in 24-hour notation. 2400 is midnight. 1200 is noon.
  - What time is 1300? 1PM
  - What time is 2300? 11PM

Fractions

Lesson 136

- Students will: find factors
- A **factor** is a number that divides evenly into a number.
  - Ask your child what are all the numbers you can multiply together to get two.
    - just 1 and 2
    - One and two are factors of two.
  - Why is one a factor of every number?
    - One is a factor of every number because you can multiply one by any number and get that number.
  - Ask your child what are all the numbers you can multiply to get to twelve.
    - 1 and 12, 2 and 6, 3 and 4
    - 1, 2, 3, 4, 6, 12 are all the factors of twelve.

- Lesson 136 worksheet
  - They will be finding factors.

Lesson 137

- Students will: reduce and simplify fractions
- Check to see if your child remembers what it means to simplify a fraction.
  - One way to simplify a fraction is to make sure it is a proper fraction.
    - What is three halves simplified?
      - Two goes into three one time with one left over. You write that 1 ½, one and one half.
      - To find that answer they can divide or subtract. Division is just subtraction over and over again. They are subtracting out $2/2$ and are left with ½. The two halves is equal to one.
    - What is seven thirds simplified?
      - Three goes into seven two times with one left over.
      - $2\,^1/_3$, two and one third
  - Another way to simplify a fraction is to reduce it, make the numbers lower by dividing the top and bottom by the same number, which is just dividing by one, keeping the fractions equal. Reducing a fraction is finding an equivalent fraction in the lowest terms.
    - What is six eighths simplified?
      - ¾, three fourths
    - What are some clues to help you reduce fractions?
      - If both the numerator and denominator are even, they can both be divided by two.
      - If they both end in zero, they can both be divided by ten.
      - If they both end in either five or zero, they can both be divided by five.
      - For other ones they should think about what the factors are of both numbers.
- Lesson 137 worksheet
  - They will simplify the fractions by converting improper fractions and reducing fractions as low as they can go. They may have to divide more than once to figure it out.

Lesson 138

- Students will: add mixed fractions and simplify the answers
- Ask your child what's one and two thirds plus one and two thirds.
  - two and four thirds
  - What's that simplified?
    - 3 1/3
    - Four thirds is one and one third. One plus one plus one and one third, is three and one third.

- They need to remember to do that when they simplify the answers today.
- Lesson 138 worksheet
  - They will be adding mixed numbers.

Lesson 139

- Students will: subtract fractions with like denominators
- Lesson 139 worksheet
  - They will subtract and simplify their answers.

Lesson 140

- Students will: subtract mixed numbers with common denominators
- There is a tricky thing in today's lesson.
- Ask your child what's three and one third minus one and two thirds.
  - What's the problem?
    - One third is less than two thirds.
- See if your child has any ideas for solving this. They have to do the opposite of simplifying an improper fraction.
  - They will take one from the three and turn it into three thirds. They are borrowing from the three. The one third becomes four thirds. Then they can subtract.
- Try this one 5 ¼ - 2 ¾.
  - $4\,{}^5/_4 - 2\,{}^3/_4 = 2\,{}^2/_4 = 2\,{}^1/_2$
- Lesson 140 worksheet
  - The extra step is just required on the problems at the bottom of the page.

Lesson 141

- Students will: add three fractions with like denominators, simplify fractions
- Lesson 141 worksheet
  - They need to simplify the fractions by changing improper fractions into mixed numbers and by reducing fractions as low as they can.

Lesson 142

- Students will: add and subtract fractions with unlike denominators
- Have your child draw two circles.
  - They should color half of one and one quarter of the other.
  - Ask them to add ½ + ¼.
    - It's not $^2/_6$. That's one third, and one half is already bigger than one third. It's not two halves, that would be one whole. It's not two fourths because that's one half and we're adding more to one half.
    - You can't do it until you have the same number of total pieces, until you have a common denominator between the two things you are adding.

EP Math 4 Parent's Guide

- Have your child draw a line across the half circle to divide it into fourths.
  - How many fourths are colored in?
    - 2
  - Now they can add 2 fourths and 1 fourth and get 3 fourths.
- That's what they are doing today. Use the worksheet to go over how to do it. They are going to find equivalent fractions where the fractions being added or subtracted both have the same denominator.
- Lesson 142 worksheet
  - Take a look at the directions together.
    - Then take a look at the examples.
    - In the first example, the best way to find a common denominator is to multiply each by the other's denominator. That way both denominators are factors.
      - It's easiest to look at the examples and walk through them.
    - In the second example, it would give you bigger numbers to work with if you just multiplied the denominators together.
      - You can notice that 4 and 6 are both factors of twelve.
        - You can turn 4 into twelve by multiplying it by 3. Multiply the top and bottom by three to get an equivalent fraction.
        - Six needs to be multiplied by two to get to twelve and the top and bottom should both be multiplied by two to get an equivalent fraction.
    - The best way to think about a problem like that is to start multiplying the larger number to see if the smaller number goes into it.
      - Four doesn't go into 6 x 1.
      - Four does go into 6 x 2.
  - Once the fractions have the same denominator, they can be subtracted or added together.

Lesson 143

- Students will: add fractions with unlike denominators
- Lesson 143 worksheet
  - They can turn back to Lesson 142 for help if they need it.
  - They need to always simplify their answers.

Lesson 144

- Students will: subtract fractions with unlike denominators
- Lesson 144 worksheet
  - They can turn back to Lesson 142 for help if they need it.
  - They need to always simplify their answers.

Lesson 145

- Students will: solve riddles, round to the nearest ten, hundred, thousand
- Lesson 145 worksheet
  - They need to pay attention to what place they are rounding to.

Lesson 146

- Students will: add fractions, simplify fractions
- Lesson 146 worksheet
  - They need to remember to always simply fractions by making sure there are no improper fractions and that the numerator and denominator are as small as they can be.

Lesson 147

- Students will: subtract fractions, simplify fractions
- Lesson 147 worksheet
  - They may need to borrow from the whole number. They can look at Lesson 140 for a reminder of how to do that.

Lesson 148

- Students will: multiply fractions, simplify fractions
- Lesson 148 worksheet
  - They can look back at Lesson 91 for help if they need it.
  - To multiply fractions you multiply the numerators together and the denominators together. Then simplify.
  - They need to divide first to make smaller numbers to multiply by, for instance, crossing off a three in both the numerator and denominator.
    - They all can be reduced in this way.

Lesson 149

- Students will: divide fractions, simplify fractions
- Lesson 149 worksheet
  - They can look back at Lesson 93 for a reminder.
  - They will multiply the first number by the reciprocal of the second number.

Lesson 150

- Students will: estimate sums
- Lesson 150 worksheet
  - They will round the numbers to the nearest hundred and add.

Lesson 151

- Students will: review with word problems
- Lesson 151 worksheet
    - There is nothing new, but you might want to read over the worksheet or have your child read it over to see if they have any questions. For instance, do they remember median and range from the average lessons?

Lesson 152

- Students will: review with word problems
- Lesson 152 worksheet

Lesson 153 (inch ruler)

- Students will: review with word problems
- Lesson 153 worksheet

Lesson 154

- Students will: review with word problems
- Lesson 154 worksheet

Lesson 155 (5 pencils and pens, a mix of both)

- Students will: review expanded and standard notation, choose likely and unlikely events
- Practice with probability.
    - Take the pencils and pens, mix them up, and lay them in a row out of the sight of your child. Have them choose a number 1to 5 and show them which one they chose.
        - Try a few times.
    - Which came up more frequently?
        - Whichever you had more of came up more frequently. You were more likely to choose it.
- Probability tells us what's likely to happen.
    - Probability would tell us that if you had one pen and four pencils and tried that experiment one hundred times, you would pick the pen 20 times and a pencil 80 times. There was an 80% chance of you choosing a pencil. There was a 20% chance of you choosing a pen. There was a 100% chance of you choosing one or the other. 20 + 80 = 100
- Lesson 155 worksheet

Order of Operations

Lesson 156

- Students will: practice addition for speed and accuracy, learn the order of operations
- Ask your child what $3 + 1 \times 2$ equals.
  - It's not 8.
  - There's something called the order of operations. It tells us in what order we need to perform the addition and subtraction and multiplication and division in a problem. The answer depends on following the correct order.
    - We multiply before we add, so the answer is 5.
- Here's the order: parentheses, exponents, multiplication and division, addition and subtraction.
  - There's a pneumonic device for this: Please Excuse My Dear Aunt Sally.
  - We solve what's in the parentheses first.
  - Then we solve multiplication and division left to right.
  - Then we solve addition and subtraction left to right.
  - We haven't used exponents yet, so you don't have to worry about those.
    - (An exponent is the little two in cm^2 and $E = mc^2$. It tells us to multiply a number by itself.)
- Try this problem the right way and by just working left to right. How different are the answers?

$$4 + 5 \times (6 - 2) =$$

  - 24 is the correct answer. Six minus two times five add four.
    - Solve the parentheses, $4 + 5 \times 4$.
    - Multiply, $4 + 20$.
    - Add, 24.
  - If you just worked left to right, the answer would be, 52!
- Here's another example.
  - $6 + 8 \div 2 \times 3 - 2$
  - No parentheses or exponents.
  - Solve multiplication and division left to right, $6 + 4 \times 3 - 2$, $6 + 12 - 2$.
  - Solve addition and subtraction left to right, $18 - 2$.
  - 16 is the answer using PEDMAS.
    - Straight forward left to right give us 19.
- Lesson 156 worksheet
  - There are addition problems they can do as quickly and accurately as possible. Time them as they work. You could tell them you'll add twenty seconds onto their time for any mistakes.
  - To complete the bottom of the page they need to follow the order of operations.
    - They could write PEMDAS on the page to help them remember.

Lesson 157

- Students will: practice subtraction for time and accuracy, solve problems following the order of operations
- Lesson 157 worksheet
  - Time them as they work on the top section. You could penalize their time for any mistakes.
  - They need to use the order of operations to figure out the bottom section. Make sure they remember what it is. You can check back at Lesson 156 for the pneumonic reminder.

Lesson 158

- Students will: practice multiplication for time and accuracy, solve problems following the order of operations
- Lesson 158 worksheet
  - Time them as they work on the top section. You could penalize their time for any mistakes.
  - They need to follow the order of operations to complete the bottom section. Make sure they remember what it is. You can check back at Lesson 156 for the pneumonic reminder.

Lesson 159

- Students will: practice division for time and accuracy, add and subtract fractions with uncommon denominators
- Lesson 159 worksheet
  - You can time the top part.
  - Ask your child if they need to review how to find equivalent fractions with common denominators.
    - They will need to find the equivalent fractions so that the denominators are the same (often by multiplying each by the other's denominator), add or subtract, then simplify.

Lesson 160

- Students will: complete arithmetic problems with fractions and decimals, calculate the percent of numbers
- Lesson 160 worksheet
  - Look at the sheet together and ask your child if they want to review any of the parts.
    - Decimals are done just like regular numbers but the same number of decimal places in the problem need to be in the answer.
    - To multiply fractions you just multiply straight across the numerator and denominator. To divide them you first switch the second number upside down to its reciprocal.

- To find the percent of a number just convert the percent to a decimal by placing a decimal point over two places 60% = .60 and then multiplying.

Coordinate Plane

Lesson 161

- Students will: write coordinates, solve four-digit addition problems with four addends
- Lesson 161 worksheet
  - Go over how to read the coordinate plane.
  - The most important thing to remember is that the horizontal value goes first.
    - Have your child identify the coordinates of a couple of the letters before you leave them to it.
      - They will look across at the numbered line it is on and then look up at what numbered line it is on.
- Continued on the next page…
  - For the addition, personally, I would allow them to do the first two and then have them checked. If they are both correct, they are done with that section. If one is wrong, they do one more. If both have a mistake, they do two more.
    - That's just a way to encourage them to be careful to not make little mistakes.

Lesson 162

- Students will: plot points on a coordinate plane, subtract four-digit numbers
- Lesson 162 worksheet
  - Again, I would allow them to complete two problems in the top section and then have them checked to see if they need to do any more.
  - In the second section, they will plot the points remembering to go across first and then up.

Lesson 163

- Students will: write coordinates, multiply four-digit numbers
- Lesson 163 worksheet
  - Same idea on this worksheet, let them prove they can do it with the top section, and this time they will be writing the coordinates for the bottom section, horizontal number first!

Lesson 164

- Students will: plot coordinates, divide two digits into four
- Lesson 164 worksheet
  - You can decide how you want to work the top section. After they plot the points on the second section, they should try to come up with three words that use all four of the letters.

Lesson 165

- Students will: read coordinates, write number words
- Lesson 165 worksheet
  - They just need to match the coordinates today. For the next part they are to write the numbers out in words. On Lesson 15 there is a page with some number words written out if they need help.

Probability

Lesson 166

- Students will: perform mental math operations, understand probability
- Lesson 166+ worksheet (mental math)
- Read the mental math problems to your child one at a time. Don't repeat.
  - How many inches are in one foot? **12 inches**
  - Write a division problem with a quotient of five. **answers will vary, 25/5**
  - Round 23 to the nearest ten. **20**
  - Solve 16 x 2. **32**
  - Which month has the fewest days? **February**
- We talked a little about probability before. Probability tells us how likely it is that something will happen.
  - If there is 0% chance of it raining today, is it going to rain?
    - No, it's not going to happen.
  - If there is a 100% chance of rain today, is it going to rain?
    - Yes, it's definitely going to happen.
  - If there is a 50% chance of something happening, what does that mean?
    - It means there is the same chance of it happening as not happening.
- Since we can talk about probability with percent, we can describe probability with fractions and decimals as well. What's 50% as a fraction and decimal?
  - ½ and 0.5
- If there were three oranges and one apple, what are the chances you'd randomly pick an apple?
  - You have a one out of four chance.
    - How is that written as a percent, decimal, fraction?
      - 25%, 0.25, ¼ One out of four is one fourth.

- That means there are four possible outcomes and one of them is the one you are looking for, called a "favorable outcome."
- Lesson 166 worksheet
  - They need to think through the answers considering what they know of 0, 50 and 100 percent chance.
  - Toward the bottom it shows how to write a fraction to show probability.
    - The numerator is how many favorable outcomes are possible.
    - The denominator is how many possible outcomes there are all together.

Lesson 167

- Students will: perform mental math operations, find probability
- Lesson 166+ worksheet (mental math)
- Read the problems to your child one time each.
  - $526 + 74 =$ **600**
  - 10 divided by 2, times 2, times 3 = **30**
  - What number is one less than 99? **98**
  - Ten minus six. Is that greater than, less than, or equal to $6 + 8$? **<**
  - Write a multiplication problem that equals 20. **answers will vary 2*10**
- Lesson 167 worksheet
  - Review probability as necessary with your child. They need to think about the outcome being asked about compared to the total number of possible outcomes. The total possible is the denominator.

Lesson 168

- Students will: perform mental math operations, find probability
- Lesson 166+ worksheet (mental math) Read them one at time without repeating.
  - Round 227 to the nearest hundred. **200**
  - 60 divided by 3 plus 3 = **23**
  - A three-sided polygon is called… **a triangle**
  - You have one dollar. You spend 60 cents. How much do you have left? **40 cents**
  - One hundred divided by twenty-five equals? **4**
- Lesson 168 worksheet
  - They will be finding probability as a fraction. They need to think about what describes 100% certainty and 0% chance.

Lesson 169

- Students will: perform mental math operations, use tree diagrams to understand the total number of choices
- Lesson 166+ worksheet (mental math)
  - Write the numeral for 730. **730**
  - What is one half of 40? **20**
  - How much is 2 quarters and 4 dimes? **90 cents**

- o Five hundred fifty-five plus four hundred forty-four. **999**
  - o Sixty times eight = **480**
- They will make a tree diagram to show the total number of choices.
  - o First you list the base number of items. Then off of each item you list each possible choice.
  - o For instance, if you had three choices of ice cream flavors and four choices of toppings, you could list: 1, 2, 3 and then off of each of those draw four lines representing the four possible toppings.
    - ▪ Each flavor could be made four different ways.
    - ▪ You can look at the diagram to see that all together there are 3 x 4 different ways to order the ice cream.
- Lesson 169 worksheet
  - o They can make a diagram of the first one. Write red, blue, green and then draw two lines off of each to show that there are two different pants that could be worn with each shirt.
    - ▪ They have 3 x 2 possible outfits, or 6.
  - o They can solve the rest with multiplication.

Lesson 170

- Students will: perform mental math operations, learn about prediction
- Lesson 166+ worksheet (mental math)
  - o Round 51 to the nearest 10. **50**
  - o 6007 – 7 = **6000**
  - o 16 plus 4 plus 36 = **56**
  - o 72 divided by 9 = **8**
  - o One times two times three times four = **24**
- A prediction is a guess about what will happen.
  - o Ask your child how they would go about making a prediction about something.
    - ▪ They need to think about what outcomes are possible and which ones are more likely to happen. Those would make the best predictions.
      - For instance, what would be their prediction about what will come up when you flip a coin one time?
        - o It's a fifty percent chance of either one. They can predict either one with the same chance of being right.
        - o Is it easier or harder to predict what number will come up on a die than heads or tails on a coin?
          - ▪ It's harder because there are more possible outcomes. There's just a one in six chance of being correct instead of a one in two chance.
- Lesson 170 worksheet

Measurement

Lesson 171

- Students will: perform mental math operations, learn about customary vs. metric measurement
- Introduce customary versus metric units of measure.
  - Customary units of measurement are what are used in America. The rest of the world uses metric. (Besides the US, only Myanmar and Liberia don't use metric, as far as I know.)
  - Metric is used in America for science.
    - It's preferred because it's much more regular.
  - Compare customary measurements such as 12 inches in a foot, 3 feet in a yard, 1760 yards in a mile to the metric measurements of 10 millimeters in a centimeter, 100 centimeters in a meter, 1000 meters in a kilometer.
    - Ones and zeros are much easier to do math with. You can see really clearly how all the measurements relate.
  - Those measurements are for distances.
    - How do you measure weight in America with customary units?
      - ounces and pounds
      - There are 16 ounces in 1 pound. How much is half a pound?
        - 8 ounces
    - Do you know the metric measures for weight?
      - gram, kilogram
      - There are 1000 grams in a kilogram just like there are 1000 meters in a kilometer.
  - Gallons measure liquids in the customary way and liters measure liquids in metric system.
  - How do you measure temperature in each system?
    - Fahrenheit is the customary unit.
      - 32 degrees is freezing; 212 degrees is boiling.
    - Celsius is the metric unit.
      - 0 degrees is freezing; 100 degrees is boiling.
        - Again, you can easily see why metric is the measurement of choice.
- Lesson 171+ worksheet (mental math) As usual, read them each one time.
  - $6 + 80 + 3000 =$ **3086**
  - 120 divided by 6 equals **20**
  - Complete each step: 8 divided by 2, minus 1, times 5 $=$ **15**
  - 254 to the nearest ten. **250**
  - $90 \times 5 =$ **450**
- Lesson 171 worksheet

Lesson 172

- Students will: perform mental math operations, practice with customary measurements
- Lesson 172 worksheet
  - They can use the conversion chart on the page to help them with the top part if needed.
  - You can consider allowing a calculator for the last problem.
- Lesson 171+ worksheet (mental math)
  - Round 121 to the nearest 100. **100**
  - What time would it be three hours after nine o'clock? **12:00**
  - Which metric unit would be best to measure your foot? **centimeters**
  - True or false: All squares are rectangles. **true**
  - 36 divided by 6 equals… **6**

Lesson 173

- Students will: perform mental math operations, learn about tools of measurement
- Lesson 173 worksheet
  - They can go ahead and try this worksheet. A beaker is a scientific liquid measuring cup.
- Lesson 171+ worksheet (mental math)
  - Do the following steps as given: 3 times 5, minus 0, plus 14. **29**
  - Estimate 88 – 42 to the nearest ten. **90 – 40 = 50**
  - Round 52,798 to the nearest thousand. **53,000**
  - 64 + 36 = **100**
  - 5 minutes before 9AM is what time? **8:55AM**

Lesson 174 (ruler)

- Students will: perform mental math operations, measure using centimeters and inches
- Lesson 174 worksheet
  - First they need to measure with the centimeter side of their ruler. They will measure to the nearest half centimeter, so their answers will either be whole numbers or end with .5 , such as 2.5 centimeters. Each little line is one millimeter, one tenth of centimeter. Halfway is five millimeters or five tenths. We write five tenths as .5 .
  - Next they will measure to the nearest inch and quarter inch. A quarter inch is $^4/_{16}$ or ¼ simplified. It can be written as a decimal as .25, so for instance, 3.25 in.
    - There are four quarters in an inch, so their answer could be a whole number, one quarter, two quarters (a half), or three quarters (.75).

- Lesson 171+ worksheet (mental math)
  - Solve $72 - 9$. **63**
  - What number is one more than 999? **1000**
  - 7 times 6 times 2 = **84**
  - In a polygon, two edges meet to form a what? **vertex, corner**
  - Bonus: March has how many days? **31**

Lesson 175

- Students will: perform mental math operations, find the volume of cuboids
- Lesson 175 worksheet
  - The formula is on the page. They can count to figure out the top, and multiply to figure out the others. They multiply the three measurements together.
  - In a cube, all three measurements are the same, so they just multiply that one number by itself three times.
    - There's an example of an exponent there, S^3. That means you multiply the length of the side by itself three times, S x S x S.
- Continued on the next page…
- Lesson 171+ worksheet (mental math)
  - What is one sixth of 54? **9**
  - How much time passes between 2:50 PM and 9 PM? **6 hours 10 minutes**
  - Multiply 5 x 6 x 10. **300**
  - A rectangle with a length of 12 inches and width of 5 inches has a perimeter of what length? **34 inches**
  - Write the numeral for one thousand nine. **1009**

Lesson 176

- Students will: read temperatures, convert between Celsius and Fahrenheit
- Lesson 176 worksheet
  - For the thermometers they need to first figure out what each line represents. Some are one, some are two, one is five.
  - For the bottom section you can allow a calculator. They will put the number given into the equation, replacing C or F with the number and then just following the order of operations to find the answer, which will be the other measurement.

Time

Lesson 177

- Students will: tell time
- Lesson 177 worksheet
  - This should just be a review of time.

Lesson 178

- Students will: convert between time measurements
- Lesson 178 worksheet
  - They will just need to use their thinking cap on these. They need to think about which should be bigger. They will multiply and divide to find the other time. You can allow a calculator on the last one.

Lesson 179

- Students will: solve word problems about elapsed time
- Lesson 179 worksheet

Lesson 180
- Students will: solve number riddles
- Lesson 180 worksheet
  - They will have to use all they learned this year to figure out these number riddles. They will also need a separate sheet of paper to do the work.
- Celebrate! You've finished Math 4!

EP Math 4

Workbook Answers

Lesson 1

Telling Time & Rounding Numbers

A. Write the time beneath each clock.

| 2:50 | 9:30 | 11:05 | 6:45 |

B. Round each number to the nearest ten. Circle the rounded number.

(50) 52 60   80 87 (90)   40 (45) 50
(10) 13 20   (60) 64 70   20 (28) 30
70 79 (80)   20 (26) 30   60 (61) 70

C. Round each number to the nearest hundred. Circle the rounded number.

100 192 (200)   (700) 749 800
400 450 (500)   300 365 (400)
(800) 834 900   200 270 (300)

Lesson 2

Time Words, Money, Place Value, & Rounding

A. Write each time in digital form.

quarter to five	4:45	half past eight	8:30
twelve o'clock	12:00	quarter to three	2:45
quarter past six	6:15	quarter past nine	9:15

B. Write the total amount for each set of coins.

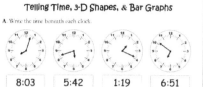

2 dimes + 7 nickels + 9 pennies = 64 ¢
2 quarters + 3 nickels + 5 pennies = 70 ¢
1 quarter + 3 dimes + 5 nickels + 7 pennies = 87 ¢

C. Write each number word as a number.

nine thousand, four hundred fifty-three = 9,453
two thousand, eight hundred thirty-one = 2,831
three thousand, seven hundred sixty-five = 3,765

D. Round each number to the nearest hundred.

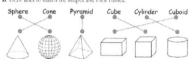

928 900   8250 8300   4492 4500
2461 2500   5743 5700   7054 7100

Lesson 3

Telling Time, 3-D Shapes, & Bar Graphs

A. Write the time beneath each clock.

| 8:03 | 5:42 | 1:19 | 6:51 |

B. Draw lines to match the shapes and their names.

Sphere   Cone   Pyramid   Cube   Cylinder   Cuboid

C. Read the double bar graph to complete the table.

Favorite Subjects
■ Boys ▨ Girls

Favorite Subjects		
Subject	Boys	Girls
Math	30	30
Art	40	20
History	10	30

Lesson 4

Telling Time & Adding 2-Digits

A. Draw the hands on each clock face to show the time.

| 12:20 | 6:05 | 9:35 | 1:50 | 10:40 |

| 1:32 | 9:41 | 11:24 | 6:58 |

B. Solve the addition problems. The first one is done for you!

59	23	74	68	49	20
+ 83	+ 74	+ 52	+ 34	+ 75	+ 35
142	97	126	102	124	55

17	54	74	37	28	58
+ 92	+ 58	+ 94	+ 86	+ 68	+ 42
109	112	168	123	96	100

Lesson 5

Fractions & Subtracting 2-Digits

A. Write the fraction that represents the shaded parts of each group.

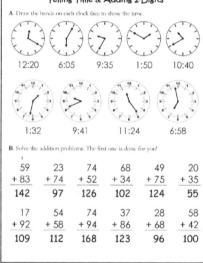

2/3   1/4
2/4   2/5
3/4   3/5
1/3   4/7

B. Solve the subtraction problems. The first one is done for you!

74	72	75	63	29	83
− 58	− 27	− 45	− 49	− 25	− 67
16	45	30	14	4	16

84	96	60	95	67	91
− 29	− 56	− 18	− 63	− 30	− 58
55	40	42	32	37	33

Lesson 6+

Daily Practice for the Week

From **Day 6** to **Day 10**, solve one set of problems each day. Time yourself!

3 x 7 = 21	6 x 8 = 48	5 x 9 = 45
8 x 4 = 32	5 x 5 = 25	4 x 6 = 24
3 x 3 = 9	9 x 9 = 81	7 x 7 = 49

28 ÷ 4 = 7	56 ÷ 7 = 8	14 ÷ 2 = 7
10 ÷ 5 = 2	18 ÷ 6 = 3	24 ÷ 3 = 8
72 ÷ 9 = 8	36 ÷ 4 = 9	81 ÷ 9 = 9

8 x 8 = 64	7 x 5 = 35	4 x 4 = 16
4 x 2 = 8	6 x 6 = 36	9 x 7 = 63
3 x 9 = 27	5 x 3 = 15	2 x 8 = 16

40 ÷ 8 = 5	42 ÷ 7 = 6	8 ÷ 1 = 8
30 ÷ 6 = 5	18 ÷ 9 = 2	20 ÷ 5 = 4
12 ÷ 3 = 4	27 ÷ 3 = 9	54 ÷ 6 = 9

Round to	Nearest 10	Nearest 100	Round to	Nearest 10	Nearest 100
35	40	0	597	600	600
974	970	1000	1012	1010	1000

Lesson 6

Adding and Subtracting Money

Add or subtract money. Don't forget the currency symbol and decimal point.

$2.00	$5.54	$8.02	$4.65
+ $3.47	+ $0.32	+ $0.16	+ $3.02
$5.47	$5.86	$8.18	$7.67

$4.13	$3.45	$2.46	$4.02
+ $4.76	+ $3.24	+ $6.23	+ $5.57
$8.89	$6.69	$8.69	$9.59

$6.72	$3.42	$2.49	$7.94
+ $2.15	+ $5.36	− $0.32	− $4.52
$8.87	$8.78	$2.17	$3.42

$8.56	$6.48	$2.96	$4.58
− $0.36	− $3.05	− $1.43	− $0.26
$8.20	$3.43	$1.53	$4.32

Pound	Euro	Chinese Yuan	Russian Ruble
£9.58	€8.64	¥9.47	₽7.63
− £3.14	− €3.42	− ¥2.17	− ₽2.20
£6.44	€5.22	¥7.30	₽5.43

Lesson 7

Estimating Sums & Adding 3-Digits

Estimate the sums by rounding the numbers to the nearest hundred. Solve the actual problems for the first four as well.

378 → 400	981 → 1000
+ 239 → + 200	+ 863 → + 900
617 600	1844 1900

453 → 500	728 → 700
+ 897 → + 900	+ 683 → + 700
1350 1400	1411 1400

638 → 600	207 → 200
+ 550 → + 600	+ 554 → + 600
estimate: 1200	estimate: 800

891 → 900	432 → 400
+ 626 → + 600	+ 237 → + 200
estimate: 1500	estimate: 600

853 → 900	950 → 1000
+ 728 → + 700	+ 394 → + 400
estimate: 1600	estimate: 1400

Lesson 8

Estimating Differences & Subtracting 3-Digits

Estimate the differences by rounding the numbers to the nearest hundred. Solve the actual problems for the first four as well.

928 → 900	647 → 600
− 529 → − 500	− 290 → − 300
399 400	357 300

896 → 900	827 → 800
− 134 → − 100	− 562 → − 600
762 800	265 200

761 → 800	743 → 700
− 438 → − 400	− 286 → − 300
estimate: 400	estimate: 400

441 → 400	835 → 800
− 373 → − 400	− 329 → − 300
estimate: 0	estimate: 500

750 → 800	881 → 900
− 195 → − 200	− 207 → − 200
estimate: 600	estimate: 700

Lesson 9

Estimating Sums & Adding 4-Digits

A. Estimate the sums by rounding the numbers to the nearest hundred.

8584 →	8600	9228 →	9200
+ 3205 →	+ 3200	+ 6150 →	+ 6200
11789	11800	15378	15400

3928 →	3900	7868 →	7900
+ 6249 →	+ 6200	+ 4762 →	+ 4800
10177	10100	12630	12700

B. Estimate the sums by rounding the numbers to the nearest thousand.

4352 →	4000	8334 →	8000
+ 6787 →	+ 7000	+ 5607 →	+ 6000
11139	11000	13941	14000

2983 →	3000	7500 →	8000
+ 6065 →	+ 6000	+ 7456 →	+ 7000
9048	9000	14956	15000

C. Choose four problems above to find the exact sums. You can solve all eight problems if you want!

Lesson 10

Estimating Differences & Subtracting 4-Digits

A. Estimate the differences by rounding the numbers to the nearest hundred.

4665 →	4700	8578 →	8600
− 1258 →	− 1300	− 4937 →	− 4900
3407	3400	3641	3700

5930 →	5900	7278 →	7300
− 1675 →	− 1700	− 3693 →	− 3700
4255	4200	3585	3600

B. Estimate the differences by rounding the numbers to the nearest thousand.

8362 →	8000	7432 →	7000
− 5756 →	− 6000	− 5867 →	− 6000
2606	2000	1565	1000

9116 →	9000	5819 →	6000
− 6569 →	− 7000	− 2982 →	− 3000
2547	2000	2837	3000

C. Choose four problems above to find the exact differences. You can solve all eight problems if you want!

Lesson 11+

Daily Practice for the Week

From **Day 11** to **Day 15**, solve one set of problems each day. Time yourself!

8 x 9 = 72	3 x 6 = 18	8 x 1 = 8
6 x 7 = 42	5 x 4 = 20	4 x 9 = 36
0 x 3 = 0	7 x 8 = 56	10 x 5 = 50
48 ÷ 6 = 8	10 ÷ 1 = 10	45 ÷ 5 = 9
35 ÷ 7 = 5	81 ÷ 9 = 9	24 ÷ 6 = 4
15 ÷ 5 = 3	25 ÷ 5 = 5	32 ÷ 8 = 4
5 x 6 = 30	8 x 3 = 24	4 x 2 = 8
2 x 9 = 18	2 x 7 = 14	9 x 6 = 54
1 x 1 = 1	5 x 8 = 40	2 x 5 = 10
27 ÷ 3 = 9	12 ÷ 2 = 6	64 ÷ 8 = 8
49 ÷ 7 = 7	36 ÷ 6 = 6	21 ÷ 3 = 7
90 ÷ 9 = 10	63 ÷ 7 = 9	16 ÷ 2 = 8
9 + 8 = 17	3 + 8 = 11	8 + 7 = 15
7 + 6 = 13	9 + 4 = 13	4 + 6 = 10
8 + 5 = 13	5 + 7 = 12	6 + 9 = 15

Lesson 11

Place Value and Expanded Notation

A. Write each number in standard form.

80 + 4 = 84	300 + 20 + 9 = 329
900 + 2 = 902	1,000 + 50 + 6 = 1,056
100 + 70 = 170	4,000 + 600 + 5 = 4,605
800 + 30 = 830	1,000 + 800 + 10 + 3 = 1,813

B. Write each number in expanded form.

42 = 40 + 2	320 = 300 + 20
56 = 50 + 6	893 = 800 + 90 + 3
105 = 100 + 5	2,017 = 2,000 + 10 + 7
3,860 =	3,000 + 800 + 60
7,428 =	7,000 + 400 + 20 + 8

C. Write each number in standard form.

five thousand, seven hundred nine	5,709
nine thousand, three hundred fifteen	9,315
two thousand, four hundred sixty-eight	2,468
eight thousand, six hundred thirty-seven	8,637

Lesson 12

Place Value and Expanded Notation

Write each number in vertically expanded form and add down the stripes.

47	92	35
4 0	9 0	3 0
+ 7	+ 2	+ 5
4 7	9 2	3 5

825	219	421
8 0 0	2 0 0	4 0 0
2 0	1 0	2 0
+ 5	+ 9	+ 1
8 2 5	2 1 9	4 2 1

5273		6452
5 0 0 0		6 0 0 0
2 0 0		4 0 0
7 0		5 0
+ 3		+ 2
5 2 7 3		6 4 5 2

Lesson 13

Place Value and Expanded Notation

A. How many hundreds, tens, and ones are in the number 405?

405 = 4 hundreds + 0 tens + 5 ones

B. Write the number 405 in expanded form, or expanded notation.

405 = 400 + 5

C. Write each number in standard form.

70 + 6 = 76	800 + 20 + 9 = 829
500 + 4 = 504	2,000 + 70 + 1 = 2,071
200 + 50 = 250	3,000 + 100 + 7 = 3,107
900 + 40 = 940	8,000 + 200 + 90 + 5 = 8,295

D. Write each number in expanded form.

82 =	80 + 2
463 =	400 + 60 + 3
305 =	300 + 5
350 =	300 + 50
5,281 =	5,000 + 200 + 80 + 1

Lesson 16+

Daily Practice for the Week

From **Day 16** to **Day 20**, solve one set of problems each day. Time yourself!

8 x 8 = 64	7 x 3 = 21	9 x 2 = 18
7 x 9 = 63	5 x 5 = 25	4 x 6 = 24
6 x 6 = 36	4 x 8 = 32	7 x 7 = 49
24 ÷ 8 = 3	10 ÷ 5 = 2	14 ÷ 2 = 7
18 ÷ 6 = 3	54 ÷ 9 = 6	20 ÷ 4 = 5
27 ÷ 3 = 9	42 ÷ 7 = 6	40 ÷ 5 = 8
7 x 5 = 35	5 x 9 = 45	2 x 6 = 12
6 x 8 = 48	3 x 3 = 9	9 x 9 = 81
3 x 5 = 15	2 x 8 = 16	7 x 8 = 56
4 ÷ 2 = 2	56 ÷ 8 = 7	36 ÷ 4 = 9
72 ÷ 8 = 9	28 ÷ 7 = 4	80 ÷ 8 = 10
10 ÷ 5 = 2	16 ÷ 2 = 8	30 ÷ 5 = 6
17 − 9 = 8	16 − 8 = 8	12 − 4 = 8
10 − 3 = 7	11 − 6 = 5	18 − 9 = 9
13 − 5 = 8	14 − 7 = 7	15 − 8 = 7

Lesson 18

Place Value to Millions

Write the value of each underlined digit in words.

ones	*tens*	ten thousands	*thousands*
hundreds	hundred thousands	*millions*	

4<u>7</u>,531	thousands
2,4<u>2</u>9	tens
1<u>9</u>,270	thousands
25,28<u>6</u>	ones
<u>6</u>3,744	ten thousands
1<u>4</u>2,625	hundred thousands
731,8<u>2</u>3	hundreds
4<u>2</u>3,212	ten thousands
2,2<u>5</u>4,065	thousands
<u>8</u>,564,159	millions
4,<u>3</u>78,387	hundred thousands

Lesson 19

Place Value to Millions

A. Write each number in expanded form.

32,917 =	30,000 + 2,000 + 900 + 10 + 7
54,890 =	50,000 + 4,000 + 800 + 90
672,039 =	600,000 + 70,000 + 2,000 + 30 + 9
2,803,426 =	2,000,000 + 800,000 + 3,000 + 400 + 20 + 6
4,367,204 =	4,000,000 + 300,000 + 60,000 + 7,000 + 200 + 4

B. Write 4-digit numbers. Then write each number in expanded form.

=

=

C. Write 5-digit numbers. Then write each number in expanded form.

=

=

Lesson 20

Place Value to Millions

A. Write each number in standard or expanded form to complete the table.

7,325	7,000 + 300 + 20 + 5
406,932	400,000 + 6,000 + 900 + 30 + 2
9,312,507	9,000,000 + 300,000 + 10,000 + 2,000 + 500 + 7

B. Write each number in standard or word form to complete the table.

12,368	twelve thousand, three hundred sixty-eight
242,719	two hundred forty-two thousand, seven hundred nineteen
4,502,587	four million, five hundred two thousand, five hundred eighty-seven

Lesson 21

Mental Math & Timed Multiplication

A. Write your answers for the Mental Math problems.

1. 60 2. 30 3. 5 4. 6
5. 25 6. 46 7. 80 8. 4

B. Multiply. Your goal should be to answer them all correctly as fast as possible. Time yourself to see how fast you can do it.

7 x 7 = 49	8 x 7 = 56	6 x 9 = 54
9 x 8 = 72	3 x 6 = 18	5 x 5 = 25
5 x 6 = 30	7 x 5 = 35	1 x 4 = 4
8 x 3 = 24	4 x 9 = 36	2 x 5 = 10
2 x 7 = 14	2 x 6 = 12	7 x 3 = 21
9 x 5 = 45	8 x 5 = 40	9 x 9 = 81
5 x 4 = 20	4 x 4 = 16	4 x 6 = 24
2 x 9 = 18	6 x 6 = 36	9 x 3 = 27
7 x 4 = 28	2 x 8 = 16	8 x 4 = 32
6 x 8 = 48	7 x 9 = 63	6 x 7 = 42
7 x 0 = 0	8 x 8 = 64	Time: _____

Lesson 22

Mental Math & Timed Division

A. Write your answers for the Mental Math problems.

1. 70 2. 30 3. 5 4. 2
5. 65 6. 3 7. 6 8. 10

B. Divide. Your goal should be to answer them all correctly as fast as possible. Time yourself to see how fast you can do it.

64 ÷ 8 = 8	54 ÷ 9 = 6	16 ÷ 2 = 8
42 ÷ 6 = 7	36 ÷ 6 = 6	45 ÷ 5 = 9
25 ÷ 5 = 5	40 ÷ 8 = 5	28 ÷ 7 = 4
72 ÷ 8 = 9	32 ÷ 1 = 32	10 ÷ 5 = 2
24 ÷ 4 = 6	18 ÷ 6 = 3	32 ÷ 4 = 8
48 ÷ 6 = 8	36 ÷ 4 = 9	49 ÷ 7 = 7
30 ÷ 5 = 6	24 ÷ 8 = 3	81 ÷ 9 = 9
16 ÷ 4 = 4	12 ÷ 6 = 2	20 ÷ 5 = 4
27 ÷ 9 = 3	35 ÷ 5 = 7	14 ÷ 2 = 7
15 ÷ 3 = 5	63 ÷ 7 = 9	56 ÷ 7 = 8
12 ÷ 4 = 3	21 ÷ 3 = 7	Time: _____

Lesson 23

Mental Math & Timed Multiplication

A. Write your answers for the Mental Math problems.

1. 90 2. 40 3. 13 4. 4
5. 50 6. 8000 7. 63 8. 85

B. Multiply. Your goal should be to answer them all correctly as fast as possible. Time yourself to see how fast you can do it.

6 x 3 = 18	7 x 2 = 14	8 x 9 = 72
8 x 8 = 64	4 x 8 = 32	3 x 3 = 9
3 x 7 = 21	5 x 1 = 5	8 x 6 = 48
4 x 2 = 8	4 x 5 = 20	9 x 7 = 63
5 x 8 = 40	6 x 2 = 12	6 x 5 = 30
0 x 3 = 0	3 x 9 = 27	7 x 6 = 42
6 x 6 = 36	4 x 7 = 28	9 x 4 = 36
5 x 7 = 35	5 x 5 = 25	7 x 7 = 49
6 x 4 = 24	9 x 6 = 54	8 x 2 = 16
3 x 8 = 24	4 x 3 = 12	5 x 9 = 45
9 x 9 = 81	7 x 8 = 56	Time: _____

Lesson 24

Mental Math & Timed Division

A. Write your answers for the Mental Math problems.

1. 70 2. 70 3. 16 4. 13
5. 400 6. 2000 7. 96 8. 346

B. Divide. Your goal should be to answer them all correctly as fast as possible. Time yourself to see how fast you can do it.

45 ÷ 9 = 5	49 ÷ 7 = 7	40 ÷ 5 = 8
36 ÷ 6 = 6	63 ÷ 9 = 7	28 ÷ 4 = 7
15 ÷ 5 = 3	18 ÷ 3 = 6	64 ÷ 8 = 8
56 ÷ 8 = 7	42 ÷ 7 = 6	14 ÷ 7 = 2
72 ÷ 9 = 8	16 ÷ 8 = 2	25 ÷ 5 = 5
21 ÷ 7 = 3	27 ÷ 3 = 9	54 ÷ 6 = 9
12 ÷ 3 = 4	24 ÷ 6 = 4	35 ÷ 7 = 5
48 ÷ 8 = 6	18 ÷ 1 = 18	32 ÷ 8 = 4
10 ÷ 2 = 5	30 ÷ 6 = 5	16 ÷ 4 = 4
24 ÷ 3 = 8	36 ÷ 9 = 4	9 ÷ 3 = 3
81 ÷ 9 = 9	20 ÷ 4 = 5	Time: _____

Lesson 25

Mental Math Strategies

A. Add or subtract mentally. Use expanded notation or rounding.

58 + 66 = 124	85 − 43 = 42
372 + 798 = 1170	525 − 456 = 69
852 + 247 = 1099	787 + 434 = 1221

B. Solve each word problem mentally.

Ron collects stamps. He collected 58 flower stamps and 46 bird stamps. How many stamps did Ron collect altogether?

104 stamps

Roger has 966 red marbles and 759 blue marbles. Mark has 834 red marbles and 763 blue marbles. Who has more marbles?

Roger

Grace had 987 smiley stickers. She gave 879 of them to her sister Angela. How many stickers does Grace have now?

108 stickers

Mia needs to solve 35 problems. She has solved 18 problems so far. How many problems does Mia still need to solve?

17 problems

Sam read 176 pages of his reading assignment last week. He read 189 pages this week. How many pages did Sam read in all?

365 pages

The candy store sold 453 candies last week. It sold 328 candies this week. How many candies did the candy store sell altogether?

781 candies

Lesson 26+

Daily Practice for the Week

From Day 26 to Day 29, solve one set of problems each day. Time yourself!

7 + 9 = 16	8 + 2 = 10	6 + 8 = 14
5 + 7 = 12	3 + 9 = 12	3 + 6 = 9
4 + 8 = 12	7 + 4 = 11	9 + 5 = 14
30 ÷ 5 = 6	56 ÷ 8 = 7	32 ÷ 4 = 8
49 ÷ 7 = 7	63 ÷ 7 = 9	25 ÷ 5 = 5
21 ÷ 3 = 7	12 ÷ 2 = 6	16 ÷ 4 = 4
36 ÷ 4 = 9	35 ÷ 5 = 7	81 ÷ 9 = 9
15 − 7 = 8	12 − 9 = 3	9 − 4 = 5
10 − 4 = 6	11 − 5 = 6	14 − 7 = 7
11 − 3 = 8	15 − 6 = 9	13 − 5 = 8
18 − 9 = 9	16 − 8 = 8	17 − 8 = 9
40 ÷ 8 = 5	28 ÷ 4 = 7	54 ÷ 9 = 6
20 ÷ 4 = 5	42 ÷ 7 = 6	36 ÷ 6 = 6
72 ÷ 8 = 9	24 ÷ 6 = 4	48 ÷ 6 = 8
15 ÷ 5 = 3	64 ÷ 8 = 8	27 ÷ 3 = 9

Lesson 26

Multiplying 2-Digits

Let's practice multiplying bigger numbers. The first two are done for you!

16	98	41	41	27
x 4	x 4	x 3	x 30	x 5
64	392	123	1230	135

81	27	39	68	50
x 6	x 3	x 2	x 5	x 4
486	81	78	340	200

52	36	96	23	34
x 4	x 7	x 8	x 2	x 9
208	252	768	46	306

Lesson 27

Multiplying 2-Digits

Let's practice multiplying bigger numbers. The first one is done for you!

78	41	27	26	24
x 20	x 23	x 65	x 35	x 42
1560	943	1755	910	1008

25	70	32	36	72
x 38	x 59	x 16	x 82	x 40
950	4130	512	2952	2880

27	54	75	27	52
x 93	x 68	x 53	x 65	x 48
2511	3672	3975	1755	2496

Lesson 28

Multiplying 2-Digits

Solve the multiplication problems.

75 x 57 **4275**	35 x 49 **1715**	42 x 68 **2856**	79 x 60 **4740**	95 x 84 **7980**
52 x 26 **1352**	88 x 37 **3256**	39 x 46 **1794**	63 x 35 **2205**	80 x 43 **3440**
10 x 72 **720**	48 x 53 **2544**	26 x 65 **1690**	29 x 75 **2175**	86 x 23 **1978**

Lesson 29

Multiplying 2-Digits

Solve the multiplication problems.

43 x 86 **3698**	90 x 57 **5130**	75 x 36 **2700**	25 x 73 **1825**	63 x 48 **3024**
28 x 65 **1820**	56 x 47 **2632**	19 x 82 **1558**	93 x 68 **6324**	79 x 30 **2370**
85 x 17 **1445**	50 x 72 **3600**	43 x 86 **3698**	92 x 55 **5060**	64 x 29 **1856**

Lesson 30

Place Value, Rounding, & Counting Money

A. Write each number in standard and expanded form to complete the table.

Standard	Expanded	Word
512	500 + 10 + 2	five hundred twelve
1,408	1,000 + 400 + 8	one thousand, four hundred eight
2,930	2,000 + 900 + 30	two thousand, nine hundred thirty

B. Round each number to the nearest ten, hundred, and thousand.

	2519	4178	5924	7352
Nearest 10	2520	4180	5920	7350
Nearest 100	2500	4200	5900	7400
Nearest 1000	3000	4000	6000	7000

C. Write the total amount for each set of bills and coins.

3 fives + 4 ones + 8 nickels + 5 dimes = **$19.90**

5 tens + 3 fives + 7 quarters + 8 pennies = **$66.83**

2 twenties + 9 fives + 3 dimes + 9 nickels = **$85.75**

4 twenties + 2 tens + 5 quarters + 6 dimes = **$101.85**

Lesson 31+

Daily Practice for the Week

From **Day 31** to **Day 35**, solve one set of problems each day. Time yourself!

8 + 7 = 15	7 + 9 = 16	5 + 8 = 13
3 + 9 = 12	4 + 7 = 11	6 + 4 = 10
7 + 6 = 13	9 + 5 = 14	10 + 9 = 19
5 x 6 = 30	9 x 4 = 36	5 x 8 = 40
6 x 9 = 54	3 x 8 = 24	4 x 7 = 28
8 x 7 = 56	7 x 6 = 42	9 x 8 = 72
15 − 7 = 8	12 − 7 = 5	16 − 8 = 8
18 − 9 = 9	10 − 9 = 1	13 − 5 = 8
11 − 6 = 5	17 − 8 = 9	14 − 6 = 8
27 ÷ 3 = 9	48 ÷ 8 = 6	45 ÷ 9 = 5
24 ÷ 6 = 4	21 ÷ 3 = 7	12 ÷ 2 = 6
32 ÷ 8 = 4	63 ÷ 7 = 9	35 ÷ 5 = 7
90 x 5 = 450	56 − 7 = 49	16 ÷ 4 = 4
17 + 7 = 24	18 ÷ 3 = 6	32 − 5 = 27
25 + 8 = 33	21 + 9 = 30	60 x 8 = 480

Lesson 31

Bar Graph & Pictograph

A. The tally chart shows the number of coins collected by Paul's coin club. Make a bar graph and a pictograph to represent the data from the tally chart.

Tally Chart	
Paul	IIII
Mia	HHII
Max	HHI
Ron	HHIII

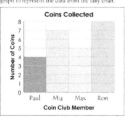

Coins Collected — Number of Coins / Coin Club Member (Paul, Mia, Max, Ron)

Name	Number of Coins
Paul	◐◐
Mia	◐◐◐◐
Max	◐◐◐
Ron	◐◐◐◐◐

KEY ◖ = 1 coin   ◯ = 2 coins

B. Make your own tally chart and bar graph using the next worksheet.

Lesson 32

Line Graph & Pie Chart

A. The table shows the number of lemonade cups Ava sold each day at her lemonade stand. Make a line graph to represent the data from the table.

# of Cups Sold	
Mon.	5
Tue.	15
Wed.	10
Thur.	20
Fri.	20

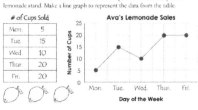

Ava's Lemonade Sales — Number of Cups / Day of the Week

B. The table shows the amount of money Ava spent for her lemonade stand. Make a pie chart, or a circle graph, to represent the data from the table.

Money Spent	
Lemons	$9
Sugar	$3
Cups	$4
Ice	$1
Napkins	$2
Other	$5

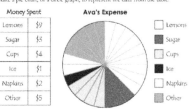

Ava's Expense — Lemons, Sugar, Cups, Ice, Napkins, Other

Lesson 33

Frequency Diagrams

Choose the correct answer for each question.

Sixteen children were asked whether they like rain. Eight children said yes. What fraction of a pie chart would be taken up by the Yes segment? — **c. one half**

In a room of 15 children, 10 were boys and 5 were girls. What fraction of a pie chart would be taken up by the Girls segment? — **b. one third**

The grocery store sold 240 boxes of cereal. On a pictograph where 1 square represents 40 boxes, how many squares would you put on the Cereal line? — **a. 6**

In a pictograph of favorite desserts, 1 circle represents 6 children. The line for cake shows 5 ½ circles. How many children prefer cake? — **b. 33**

Adam surveyed his 12 friends and drew a bar graph to show their favorite colors. There was no bar above the label Purple. How many friends prefer purple? — **a. 0**

Which of these would be best at showing how the number of division problems you solve in 3 minutes changes over time during the year? — **b. line graph**

Tally marks are usually drawn in groups of — **b. 5**

Lesson 34

Double-Line Graphs

The double-line graph shows the amount of money Olivia and Abby spent in 7 months. Use the graph to answer the questions.

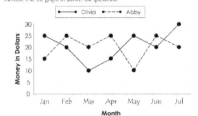

Olivia ●——● Abby — Money in Dollars / Month (Jan, Feb, Mar, Apr, May, Jun, Jul)

1. How much did Abby spend in total? — **$140**

2. How much money was spent by both in March? — **$30**

3. How much more did Olivia spend than Abby in May? — **$15**

4. How many months did Abby spend more than Olivia? — **4 months**

5. Who spent more money in total? — **Olivia**

Lesson 35

Counting Money & Telling Time

A. Choose True or False for each statement. Try to calculate mentally.

Kate has 39 cents less than Justin. If Kate has 45 cents, Justin must have 86 cents. — True **False**

Eric bought 2 bags of chips. Each bag was 37 cents. Eric paid less than 84 cents. — **True** False

Brian has six coins worth fifty-five cents. If five of his coins are nickels, the other must be a quarter. — True **False**

Orson has 3 dimes, 9 nickels, 1 quarter, and 6 pennies. Laura has 5 nickels, 2 quarters, 3 pennies, and 2 dimes. Orson has less money than Laura. — True **False**

B. Write the time beneath each clock.

9:40   2:20   12:30   6:45   11:50

5:05   8:35   10:15   11:10   5:20

Lesson 36+

Daily Practice for the Week

From **Day 36** to **Day 40**, solve one set of problems each day. Time yourself!

18 + 6 = 24	8 + 14 = 22	19 + 17 = 36
15 + 9 = 24	7 + 15 = 22	15 + 13 = 28
16 + 4 = 20	9 + 19 = 28	14 + 18 = 32
2 x 5 = 10	8 x 3 = 24	9 x 6 = 54
5 x 8 = 40	9 x 4 = 36	2 x 9 = 18
3 x 6 = 18	7 x 2 = 14	4 x 7 = 28
14 – 7 = 7	12 – 8 = 4	20 – 12 = 8
16 – 9 = 7	17 – 4 = 13	19 – 17 = 2
18 – 3 = 15	15 – 7 = 8	10 – 10 = 0
35 ÷ 5 = 7	72 ÷ 9 = 8	63 ÷ 7 = 9
27 ÷ 3 = 9	48 ÷ 8 = 6	32 ÷ 4 = 8
56 ÷ 8 = 7	36 ÷ 6 = 6	21 ÷ 3 = 7
18 + 5 = 23	20 – 7 = 13	49 ÷ 7 = 7
30 x 6 = 180	24 ÷ 6 = 4	12 + 8 = 20
12 – 7 = 5	11 – 9 = 2	40 x 8 = 320

Lesson 36

Multiplying 3-Digits

Solve the multiplication problems. Two problems are done for you!

875	616	411	251
x 6	x 4	x 56	x 98
5,250	2,464	23,016	24,598

746	362	147	950
x 58	x 68	x 95	x 27
43,268	24,616	13,965	25,650

906	578	482	326
x 43	x 34	x 91	x 27
38,958	19,652	43,862	8,802

Lesson 37

Multiplying 3-Digits

Solve the multiplication problems. The first one is done for you!

475	384	481	762
x 381	x 259	x 596	x 873
180,975	99,456	286,676	665,226

124	942	47	84
x 56	x 74	x 93	x 25
6,944	69,708	4,371	2,100

Lesson 38

Multiplying 3-Digits

Solve the multiplication problems.

720	495	787	538
x 532	x 253	x 321	x 694
383,040	125,235	252,627	373,372

578	810	452	293
x 975	x 641	x 930	x 382
563,550	519,210	420,360	111,926

Lesson 39

Multiplying 3-Digits

Solve the multiplication problems.

201	392	800	476
x 374	x 549	x 270	x 305
75,174	215,208	216,000	145,180

391	125	820	564
x 367	x 746	x 342	x 486
143,497	93,250	280,440	274,104

Lesson 40

Reading Tables, Rounding, & Place Value

A. Read the table to fill in the blanks.

Class	# Boys	# Girls
1st Grade	10	14
2nd Grade	8	12
3rd Grade	15	13
4th Grade	11	9

There are **24** kids in 1st Grade.

2nd Grade has **4** more girls than boys.

3rd Grade has **8** more kids than 4th.

There are **92** kids in total.

3rd and 4th Grade have **8** more boys than 1st and 2nd Grade.

B. Round each number to the nearest ten, hundred, and thousand.

	3641	1387	6835	8020
Nearest 10	3640	1390	6840	8020
Nearest 100	3600	1400	6800	8000
Nearest 1000	4000	1000	7000	8000

C. Write each number in standard form.

40 + 5 = **45**   1,000 + 30 + 4 = **1,034**

200 + 70 = **170**   8,000 + 600 + 9 = **8,609**

600 + 20 = **620**   5,000 + 200 + 10 + 7 = **5,217**

Lesson 41+

Daily Practice for the Week

From **Day 41** to **Day 45**, solve one set of problems each day. Time yourself!

12 + 6 = 18	7 + 15 = 22	14 + 17 = 31
18 + 7 = 25	3 + 14 = 17	16 + 18 = 34
15 + 9 = 24	9 + 18 = 27	11 + 19 = 30
7 x 8 = 56	6 x 7 = 42	9 x 9 = 81
6 x 9 = 54	4 x 8 = 32	5 x 4 = 20
4 x 4 = 16	5 x 6 = 30	8 x 6 = 48
14 – 8 = 6	12 – 9 = 3	20 – 17 = 3
16 – 7 = 9	17 – 2 = 15	19 – 12 = 7
11 – 5 = 6	13 – 8 = 5	15 – 10 = 5
36 ÷ 6 = 6	45 ÷ 9 = 5	25 ÷ 5 = 5
64 ÷ 8 = 8	10 ÷ 5 = 2	63 ÷ 7 = 9
12 ÷ 3 = 4	49 ÷ 7 = 7	28 ÷ 4 = 7
35 ÷ 7 = 5	13 – 6 = 7	40 ÷ 5 = 8
90 x 8 = 720	16 + 9 = 25	50 x 3 = 150
12 – 5 = 7	24 ÷ 4 = 6	19 + 4 = 23

Lesson 41

Multiplying 2-Digits

Solve the multiplication problems.

31	46	34	57	48
x 7	x 8	x 9	x 5	x 0
217	368	306	285	0

50	84	17	95	63
x 8	x 2	x 1	x 6	x 7
400	168	17	570	441

61	39	58	82	71
x 9	x 7	x 3	x 4	x 3
549	273	174	328	213

Lesson 42

Multiplying 2-Digits

Solve the multiplication problems.

20	15	54	63	23
x 42	x 38	x 41	x 25	x 94
840	570	2214	1575	2162

34	95	48	21	86
x 22	x 85	x 73	x 60	x 36
748	8075	3504	1260	3096

50	16	62	39	87
x 92	x 73	x 49	x 52	x 29
4600	1168	3038	2028	2523

Lesson 43

Multiplying 3-Digits

Solve the multiplication problems.

511 x 73 37,303	830 x 19 15,770	489 x 65 31,785	574 x 61 35,014
604 x 28 16,912	427 x 67 28,609	509 x 52 26,468	781 x 90 70,290
895 x 81 72,495	248 x 43 10,664	758 x 66 50,028	677 x 29 19,633

Lesson 44

Multiplying 3-Digits

Solve the multiplication problems.

908 x 122 110,776	786 x 195 153,270	357 x 774 276,318	569 x 665 378,385
914 x 558 510,012	306 x 392 119,952	832 x 747 621,504	138 x 376 51,888
316 x 806 254,696	643 x 311 199,973	419 x 570 238,830	845 x 432 365,040

Lesson 45

Estimating Products

A. Estimate each product by rounding the top number to the nearest hundred and the bottom number to the nearest ten and then multiplying the first digits.

458 → 500 x 34 → x 30 estimate: 15,000	325 → 300 x 49 → x 50 estimate: 15,000
913 → 900 x 54 → x 50 estimate: 45,000	769 → 800 x 86 → x 90 estimate: 72,000
521 → 500 x 87 → x 90 estimate: 45,000	850 → 900 x 93 → x 90 estimate: 81,000
926 → 900 x 11 → x 10 estimate: 9,000	392 → 400 x 35 → x 40 estimate: 16,000

B. Estimate the product by rounding the first number to the nearest thousand and the second number to the nearest hundred.

5,678 x 504 = **6000** x **500** = **3,000,000**

Lesson 46+

Daily Practice for the Week

From **Day 46** to **Day 50**, solve one set of problems each day. Time yourself!

15 + 5 = 20	7 + 16 = 23	19 + 15 = 34
18 + 6 = 24	5 + 18 = 23	17 + 18 = 35
17 + 5 = 22	9 + 16 = 25	16 + 15 = 31
4 x 8 = 32	7 x 7 = 49	5 x 9 = 45
5 x 7 = 35	6 x 5 = 30	8 x 7 = 56
9 x 4 = 36	8 x 9 = 72	5 x 3 = 15
16 − 7 = 9	10 − 2 = 8	12 − 9 = 3
13 − 8 = 5	14 − 7 = 7	19 − 5 = 14
11 − 3 = 8	18 − 9 = 9	20 − 6 = 14
63 ÷ 7 = 9	40 ÷ 8 = 5	28 ÷ 7 = 4
18 ÷ 6 = 3	27 ÷ 3 = 9	20 ÷ 4 = 5
24 ÷ 3 = 8	36 ÷ 6 = 6	54 ÷ 9 = 6
60 x 4 = 240	16 + 6 = 22	20 x 7 = 140
42 ÷ 6 = 7	17 − 8 = 9	17 + 9 = 26
15 − 7 = 8	81 ÷ 9 = 9	48 ÷ 6 = 8

Lesson 46

Estimating Products

A. Estimate each product by rounding the top number to the nearest hundred and the bottom number to the nearest ten and then multiplying the first digits. Solve the actual problems as well.

433 → 400 x 38 → x 40 16,454 16,000	321 → 300 x 14 → x 10 4,494 3,000
797 → 800 x 53 → x 50 42,241 40,000	704 → 700 x 62 → x 60 43,648 42,000

B. Find the difference between the actual and the estimated answers.

16,454 −16,000 454	4,494 − 3,000 1,494	42,241 −40,000 2,241	43,648 −42,000 1,648

Lesson 47

Word Problems

Solve each word problem. Use the space on the right for your work area.

Larry has 14 pairs of blue socks. How many individual socks does he have?

28 individual socks

Emma baked 28 cookies and put them equally into 4 boxes. How many cookies does each box have?

7 cookies

The worksheet has 6 rows of 6 problems in each row. How many problems are in the worksheet?

36 problems

Claire can solve 3 word problems per minute. How many word problems can she solve in 5 minutes?

15 problems

A box of books weighs 24 pounds. Each book weighs 3 pounds. How many books are in the box?

8 books

At a grocery, Ron bought 4 bags of apples and 6 jars of apple jam. Each bag of apples cost $3. Each jar cost $5. How much did Ron spend in all?

42 dollars

Lesson 48

Word Problems

Solve each word problem. Use the space on the right for your work area.

Mia has to pack 45 apples into bags. Each bag holds 8 apples. How many bags will Mia need?

6 bags

A group of 11 girls and 9 boys are on a canoe trip. Each canoe can hold 3 people. How many canoes will the group need?

7 canoes

Brian has to pack 16 math books and 27 science books into boxes. Each box can hold 5 books. How many boxes will Brian need?

9 boxes

There are 38 people going to a movie. Each car can hold 6 people. What is the fewest number of cars needed?

7 cars

There were 28 kids at Olivia's party. Mom baked 5 pies and sliced each pie into 6 pieces. Each kid had one piece of pie. How many pieces were left?

2 pieces

A recipe calls for 8 apples to make one apple pie. Angela wants to bake 6 pies. She has 53 apples. How many apples will not be used?

5 apples

Lesson 49

Word Problems

Solve each word problem. Use the space on the right for your work area.

Lucy has 35 marbles. Carrie has 19 more marbles than Lucy. How many marbles does Carrie have?

54 marbles

There are 5 boys and 6 girls. Each boy has 11 pennies and each girl has 12 pennies. How many pennies do the children have altogether?

127 pennies

Thomas has 90 cents. He wants to buy 5 candy bars. Each candy bar costs 13 cents. How much money will Thomas have left?

25 cents

Ron has 45 marbles. Matt has 18 more marbles than Ron. Naomi has 24 fewer marbles than Matt. How many marbles does Naomi have?

39 marbles

At a neighbor's garage sale, Marie bought 7 chairs. Each chair cost 13 dollars. How much money did Marie spend in total?

91 dollars

Derek has 14 stickers. Sam has 5 times as many stickers as Derek but only half as many stickers as Abby. How many stickers does Abby have?

140 stickers

Lesson 50

Word Problems

Solve each word problem. Use the space on the right for your work area.

Jim and Tom have 27 marbles. Tom has half as many as Jim. How many marbles does Tom have?

9 marbles

A recipe calls for 6 apples to make one apple pie. Mom wants to bake 5 pies. Apples are sold in bags of 8. How many bags does she need to buy?

4 bags

At an apple farm, Leah picked 3 times as many apples as Amy. Leah picked 15 apples. How many apples did they pick altogether?

20 apples

Ava has $15. Her weekly allowance is $8. How many weeks will it take her to save for a video game that costs $55?

5 weeks

Dylan spent $47 to order some tickets online. Each ticket cost $6. The shipping cost per order was $5. How many tickets did Dylan buy?

7 tickets

Matt has 6 times as many pennies as Henry and 4 times as many as Ella. Matt has 24 pennies. How many pennies do they have altogether?

34 pennies

Lesson 51

Equivalent Fractions

A. Find the equivalent fractions. Use the shapes below to help you.

$$\frac{1}{2} = \frac{2}{4} \qquad \frac{1}{3} = \frac{2}{6} \qquad \frac{1}{4} = \frac{2}{8} \qquad \frac{1}{2} = \frac{3}{6}$$

$$\frac{1}{2} = \frac{4}{8} \qquad \frac{2}{3} = \frac{8}{12} \qquad \frac{3}{4} = \frac{9}{12} \qquad \frac{5}{6} = \frac{10}{12}$$

B. Find the equivalent fractions by multiplying or dividing the top and bottom numbers (the numerator and the denominator) by the same amount.

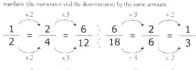

Lesson 52

Equivalent Fractions

A. Find the equivalent fractions that represent each shaded portion.

$$\frac{1}{2} = \frac{2}{4} \qquad\qquad \frac{2}{3} = \frac{4}{6}$$

$$\frac{3}{4} = \frac{6}{8} \qquad\qquad \frac{3}{5} = \frac{6}{10}$$

$$\frac{2}{6} = \frac{4}{12} \qquad\qquad \frac{1}{2} = \frac{3}{6}$$

$$\frac{1}{3} = \frac{3}{9} \qquad\qquad \frac{2}{4} = \frac{6}{12}$$

$$\frac{2}{5} = \frac{6}{15} \qquad\qquad \frac{5}{6} = \frac{15}{18}$$

B. Draw lines to match the equivalent fractions.

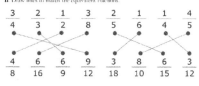

Lesson 53

Comparing Fractions

A. Compare the fractions by looking at their numerators using <, >, or =.

$$\frac{3}{4} > \frac{1}{4} \qquad \frac{5}{8} < \frac{6}{8} \qquad \frac{5}{7} = \frac{5}{7}$$

$$\frac{4}{11} < \frac{6}{11} \qquad \frac{1}{5} > \frac{0}{5} \qquad \frac{2}{9} < \frac{4}{9}$$

B. Circle the largest fraction in each set.

$$\frac{1}{8} \quad \frac{3}{6} \quad \frac{2}{5} \quad \boxed{\frac{6}{7}} \qquad\qquad \frac{1}{2} \quad \frac{4}{5} \quad \boxed{\frac{5}{6}} \quad \frac{2}{9}$$

$$\frac{2}{7} \quad \frac{1}{3} \quad \boxed{\frac{3}{4}} \quad \frac{5}{8} \qquad\qquad \frac{1}{5} \quad \boxed{\frac{3}{8}} \quad \frac{1}{4} \quad \frac{2}{7}$$

$$\frac{1}{3} \quad \frac{5}{9} \quad \frac{2}{3} \quad \boxed{\frac{7}{9}} \qquad\qquad \frac{2}{4} \quad \frac{5}{8} \quad \frac{3}{4} \quad \boxed{\frac{7}{8}}$$

Lesson 54

Fraction Word Problems

For each word problem, make a labeled sketch and write an equation. Explain your answer to someone. The first one is done for you!

After school, Adam spent $\frac{1}{4}$ of an hour on math, $\frac{1}{4}$ on reading, and $\frac{1}{4}$ on science. What fraction of an hour did he spend on studying?

Labeled Sketch: Equation:

math reading science

$$\frac{1}{4} + \frac{1}{4} + \frac{1}{4} = \frac{3}{4}$$

Kyle had $\frac{5}{6}$ of a carton of eggs. After he used some to bake cookies, $\frac{1}{6}$ of the carton was left. What fraction of the carton did Kyle use?

Labeled Sketch: Equation:

Left   Used

$$\frac{5}{6} - \frac{1}{6} = \frac{4}{6}$$

The morning break lasts $\frac{5}{8}$ of an hour. Danny spent $\frac{2}{8}$ of an hour jumping rope. What fraction of an hour did he have left after that?

Labeled Sketch: Equation:

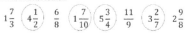

Left   Spent

$$\frac{5}{8} - \frac{2}{8} = \frac{3}{8}$$

Lesson 55

Proper Fractions

A. A proper fraction is a fraction where the numerator (the top number) is less than the denominator (the bottom number). Circle the proper fractions.

$$\frac{4}{2} \quad \boxed{\frac{2}{5}} \quad \frac{8}{6} \quad \frac{11}{11} \quad \boxed{\frac{5}{7}} \quad \boxed{\frac{3}{9}} \quad \frac{15}{10} \quad \boxed{\frac{1}{6}}$$

$$\frac{12}{16} \quad \frac{7}{3} \quad \frac{20}{10} \quad \boxed{\frac{2}{4}} \quad \frac{30}{15} \quad \boxed{\frac{4}{6}} \quad \frac{8}{8} \quad \boxed{\frac{9}{15}}$$

B. The reciprocal of a fraction is the fraction turned upside down. Circle the fractions whose reciprocal is a proper fraction.

$$\frac{12}{10} \quad \frac{3}{3} \quad \frac{5}{4} \quad \frac{21}{10} \quad \frac{1}{9} \quad \frac{6}{3} \quad \frac{15}{60} \quad \frac{8}{7}$$

C. Circle the statements whose answers give a proper fraction.

$$\frac{1}{4} + \frac{2}{4} \qquad \frac{2}{7} + \frac{5}{7} \qquad \boxed{\frac{7}{5} - \frac{4}{5}} \qquad \frac{1}{2} + \frac{1}{2}$$

$$\frac{7}{3} - \frac{2}{3} \qquad \boxed{\frac{3}{9} + \frac{4}{9}} \qquad \frac{6}{8} + \frac{3}{8} \qquad \boxed{\frac{2}{6} + \frac{1}{6}}$$

$$\boxed{\frac{1}{8} + \frac{5}{8}} \qquad \frac{9}{4} - \frac{5}{4} \qquad \boxed{\frac{3}{7} + \frac{2}{7}} \qquad \frac{5}{9} - \frac{2}{9}$$

Lesson 56

Improper Fractions

A. An improper fraction is a fraction where the numerator is greater than or equal to the denominator. Circle the improper fractions.

$$\boxed{\frac{6}{5}} \quad \frac{2}{3} \quad \frac{2}{10} \quad \boxed{\frac{15}{9}} \quad \frac{2}{8} \quad \boxed{\frac{8}{7}} \quad \boxed{\frac{15}{15}} \quad \frac{4}{6}$$

$$\boxed{\frac{4}{2}} \quad \boxed{\frac{8}{8}} \quad \frac{1}{5} \quad \frac{5}{7} \quad \boxed{\frac{12}{6}} \quad \frac{3}{4} \quad \frac{7}{10} \quad \boxed{\frac{5}{3}}$$

B. The reciprocal of a fraction is the fraction turned upside down. Circle the fractions whose reciprocal is an improper fraction.

$$\boxed{\frac{4}{12}} \quad \boxed{\frac{9}{8}} \quad \frac{10}{4} \quad \boxed{\frac{3}{7}} \quad \frac{5}{2} \quad \boxed{\frac{9}{9}} \quad \boxed{\frac{30}{20}} \quad \frac{2}{8}$$

C. Circle the statements whose answers give an improper fraction.

$$\boxed{\frac{1}{2} + \frac{1}{2}} \qquad \frac{2}{9} + \frac{3}{9} \qquad \frac{2}{6} + \frac{3}{6} \qquad \boxed{\frac{5}{8} + \frac{6}{8}}$$

$$\boxed{\frac{5}{7} + \frac{3}{7}} \qquad \frac{2}{4} + \frac{1}{4} \qquad \boxed{\frac{3}{5} + \frac{4}{5}} \qquad \frac{1}{3} + \frac{1}{3}$$

$$\frac{1}{5} + \frac{2}{5} \qquad \boxed{\frac{7}{8} + \frac{5}{8}} \qquad \frac{1}{7} + \frac{4}{7} \qquad \boxed{\frac{7}{9} + \frac{4}{9}}$$

Lesson 57

Mixed Numbers

A. A mixed fraction, or a mixed number, is a whole number and a proper fraction combined. Make mixed numbers.

B. Circle the mixed numbers.

$$1\frac{7}{3} \quad \boxed{4\frac{1}{2}} \quad \frac{6}{8} \quad \boxed{1\frac{7}{10}} \quad \boxed{5\frac{3}{4}} \quad \frac{11}{9} \quad \boxed{3\frac{2}{7}} \quad 2\frac{9}{8}$$

C. Convert between improper fractions and mixed numbers.

$$\frac{17}{3} = 5\frac{2}{3} \qquad \frac{39}{8} = 4\frac{7}{8} \qquad 7\frac{2}{9} = \frac{65}{9}$$

$$\frac{25}{4} = 6\frac{1}{4} \qquad \frac{43}{5} = 8\frac{3}{5} \qquad 2\frac{5}{7} = \frac{19}{7}$$

D. Circle the statements whose answers can be expressed as a mixed number.

$$\frac{2}{8} + \frac{3}{8} \qquad \frac{5}{7} + \frac{1}{7} \qquad \boxed{\frac{4}{9} + \frac{8}{9}} \qquad \boxed{\frac{4}{5} + \frac{7}{5}}$$

Lesson 58

Fraction Word Problems

For each word problem, make a labeled sketch and write an equation. Explain your answer to someone.

The store had $\frac{5}{6}$ of a box of apples. It sold $\frac{3}{6}$ of the box in the morning. What fraction of the box did the store have left after that?

Labeled Sketch: Equation:

Left   Sold

$$\frac{5}{6} - \frac{3}{6} = \frac{2}{6}$$

Walter bought three boxes of fruit. They weigh $1\frac{2}{6}$ pounds, $1\frac{2}{6}$ pounds, and $2\frac{1}{6}$ pounds. What is the total weight of the three boxes?

Labeled Sketch: Equation:

$$1\frac{2}{6} + 1\frac{2}{6} + 2\frac{1}{6} = 4\frac{5}{6}$$

Tracy used $1\frac{2}{8}$ gallons of red paint, $2\frac{1}{8}$ gallons of blue paint, and $2\frac{3}{8}$ gallons of white paint to paint her house. How many gallons of paint did Tracy use in total?

Labeled Sketch: Equation:

$$1\frac{2}{8} + 2\frac{1}{8} + 2\frac{3}{8} = 5\frac{6}{8}$$

Lesson 59

Fraction Word Problems

For each word problem, make a labeled sketch and write an equation. Explain your answer to someone. The first one is done for you!

The city has a beautiful 2 mile trail. Claire walked the first $1\frac{1}{4}$ miles of the trail and ran the rest. How far did she run?

Labeled Sketch: Equation:

$$2 - 1\frac{1}{4} = \frac{3}{4}$$

Matt went for a walk on the trail. He walked $\frac{3}{4}$ of a mile. Then he turned around and walked back to the start of the trail. How many miles did he walk in all?

Labeled Sketch: Equation:

$$\frac{3}{4} + \frac{3}{4} = \frac{6}{4} = 1\frac{2}{4}$$

Jacob decided to run the whole trail. After running $1\frac{3}{8}$ miles, he got tired and decided to walk the rest. How far did he have to walk to finish the trail?

Labeled Sketch: Equation:

$$2 - 1\frac{3}{8} = \frac{5}{8}$$

Lesson 60

Fraction Word Problems

For each word problem, make a labeled sketch and write an equation. Explain your answer to someone.

Chris went for a walk on the trail. He walked $1\frac{1}{8}$ of a mile. Then he turned around and walked back to the start. How many miles did he walk in all?

Labeled Sketch:

Equation:

$1\frac{1}{8} + 1\frac{1}{8} = 2\frac{2}{8}$

Laura ran to the $\frac{3}{4}$ mile marker and ran back to the $\frac{1}{4}$ mile marker. Then she turned around and ran the rest of the trail. How many miles did she run in all?

Labeled Sketch:

Equation:

$\frac{3}{4} + \frac{2}{4} + 1\frac{3}{4} = 3$

Everyday Justin walks the trail. When he gets to the $1\frac{1}{2}$ mile marker, he turns around and walks back to the start. How many miles does he walk in 5 days?

Labeled Sketch:

Equation:

$2\frac{2}{4} + 2\frac{2}{4} + 2\frac{2}{4} + 2\frac{2}{4} + 2\frac{2}{4} = 12\frac{2}{4}$

per day

Lesson 61

Division Terms

A. Let's practice three ways of writing division problems. Complete the table.

using a division symbol	using a long division symbol	as a fraction
$12 \div 3 = 4$	$3\overline{)12}$ 4	$\frac{12}{3} = 4$
$35 \div 5 = 7$	$5\overline{)35}$ 7	$\frac{35}{5} = 7$
$72 \div 8 = 9$	$8\overline{)72}$ 9	$\frac{72}{8} = 9$

B. Cut out the **Division Terms** pieces from **Day 61'**. Read their definitions below. Glue each piece over the number that matches the definition.

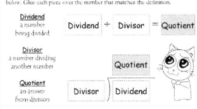

Dividend
a number being divided

Dividend ÷ Divisor = Quotient

Divisor
a number dividing another number

Quotient

Quotient
an answer from division

Divisor) Dividend

C. Read about long division on the next three worksheets.

Lesson 62

Long Division Steps II

B. Cut out the **Long Division Steps** pieces from **Day 61'**. Understand each step, glue the corresponding step piece, and explain the step in words.

$2\overline{)68}$ 3 ÷   Divide …

$2\overline{)68}$ 3 6 ✕   Multiply …

$2\overline{)68}$ 3 6 0 —   Subtract …

$2\overline{)68}$ 3 6 08 ↓   Bring down …

$2\overline{)68}$ 34 6 08 8 0 ↻   Repeat …

Lesson 63

Related Multiplication and Division

A. Solve each word problem. Use the space on the right for your work area.

Mia has 5 boxes of cookies. Each box contains 8 cookies. How many cookies does Mia have?

40 cookies

Emma puts 40 cookies equally into 5 boxes. How many cookies are in each box?

8 cookies

B. Multiplication and division are inverse operations. Use the three numbers to write related multiplication and division facts. The first one is done for you!

8, 5, 40	3, 9, 27	7, 9, 63
$8 \times 5 = 40$	$3 \times 9 = 27$	$7 \times 9 = 63$
$5 \times 8 = 40$	$9 \times 3 = 27$	$9 \times 7 = 63$
$40 \div 5 = 8$	$27 \div 9 = 3$	$63 \div 9 = 7$
$40 \div 8 = 5$	$27 \div 3 = 9$	$63 \div 7 = 9$

C. Circle the quotient in the division problem. Show how you know the answer is correct.

$2\overline{)68}$ 34

How do you check the answer?

$2 \times 34 = 68$

Lesson 64

Dividing by 1-Digit

Cut out the **Numbers** pieces from **Day 61'**. For each division equation, place the pieces to "write" a long division problem and "solve" it! Check your answer using multiplication. If the answer is correct, glue the pieces.

$84 \div 4$ $84 \div 6$

$4\overline{)84}$ 21 8 04 4 0

$6\overline{)84}$ 14 6 24 24 0

Check your answer:

$4 \times 21 = 84$ $6 \times 14 = 84$

Lesson 65

Dividing by 1-Digit

A. Find the quotient for each division problem.

$7\overline{)448}$ 64 $4\overline{)156}$ 39 $6\overline{)264}$ 44 $8\overline{)168}$ 21

B. Solve each word problem.

✓ Rebekah puts 48 apples equally into 6 baskets. How many apples will be in each basket?   **8 apples**

✓ The teacher divides 35 students into groups of 7. How many groups will be made?   **5 groups**

✓ Braden divides 28 bananas equally into 4 piles. How many bananas will be in each pile?   **7 bananas**

✓ Briley puts 49 cookies equally into 7 boxes. How many cookies are in each box?   **7 cookies**

✓ Matthew read a 180 page book. He read the same number of pages for 9 days. How many pages did he read each day?   **20 pages**

Lesson 66

Dividing with Remainders

A. Find the quotient and remainder for each division problem. Express your answer as a fraction. Check the answer using multiplication and addition.

$7 \div 2 = 3\,R\,1 = 3\frac{1}{2} \Rightarrow 2 \times 3 + 1 = 7$

$19 \div 5 = 3\,R\,4 = 3\frac{4}{5} \Rightarrow 5 \times 3 + 4 = 19$

$46 \div 7 = 6\,R\,4 = 6\frac{4}{7} \Rightarrow 7 \times 6 + 4 = 46$

B. Solve each word problem. Use the space on the right for your work area.

Sixteen apples are shared equally among 6 children. How many apples does each child get?

2 4/6 apples

Eight children share 30 cookies equally. How many cookies does each child get?

3 6/8 cookies

Nine children share a box of cherries equally. Each gets 8 cherries. There are then 5 cherries left. How many cherries were originally in the box?

77 cherries

Lesson 67

Dividing by 1-Digit

Find the quotient, and write the reminder as a fraction.

$4\overline{)138}$ $34\frac{2}{4}$ $3\overline{)784}$ $261\frac{1}{3}$ $6\overline{)953}$ $158\frac{5}{6}$ $2\overline{)629}$ $314\frac{1}{2}$

$5\overline{)759}$ $151\frac{4}{5}$ $6\overline{)325}$ $54\frac{1}{6}$ $4\overline{)565}$ $141\frac{1}{4}$ $7\overline{)885}$ $126\frac{3}{7}$

Lesson 68

Dividing by 2-Digits

A. Find the quotient, and write the remainder with an R.

$22\overline{)330}$ 15 $36\overline{)472}$ $13\,R\,4$ $41\overline{)944}$ $23\,R\,1$ $12\overline{)336}$ 28

B. Solve each word problem.

Sixteen children share 64 marbles equally. How many marbles does each child get?

4 marbles

The librarian puts 360 books equally on 10 shelves. How many books are on each shelf?

36 books

Thirteen friends bought movie tickets. They paid $117 in total. How much does each ticket cost?

9 dollars

Lesson 69

Dividing by 2-Digits

Find the quotient for each division problem.

$$5\overline{)2505} = 501 \qquad 8\overline{)1488} = 186 \qquad 6\overline{)2562} = 427 \qquad 9\overline{)7164} = 796$$

$$25\overline{)325} = 13 \qquad 24\overline{)984} = 41 \qquad 17\overline{)833} = 49 \qquad 22\overline{)968} = 44$$

YOUR WORK AREA

Lesson 70

Dividing by 2-Digits

Find the quotient and remainder for each division problem.

A	B	C	D
$87\overline{)6459}$	$96\overline{)2092}$	$20\overline{)9488}$	$32\overline{)7903}$

A = 74 R 21   C = 474 R 8

B = 21 R 76   D = 246 R 31

E	F	G	H
$25\overline{)6017}$	$75\overline{)8323}$	$12\overline{)9474}$	$53\overline{)1193}$

E = 240 R 17   G = 789 R 6

F = 110 R 73   H = 22 R 27

YOUR WORK AREA

Lesson 71

Decimal Place Value

A. Make a number using each set of place values.

7 Tens	5 Hundreds	6 Thousands
1 One	2 Tens	3 Hundreds
4 Tenths	0 Ones	4 Tens
3 Hundredths	8 Tenths	9 Ones
5 Thousandths	4 Hundredths	2 Tenths
71.435	520.84	6,349.2

5 Tens	0 Ones	3 Tenths
6 Hundredths	2 Thousands	4 Tens
3 Hundreds	1 Ten	8 Thousandths
0 Tenths	8 Tenths	2 Hundredths
3 Ones	4 Hundreds	6 Ones
353.06	2,410.8	46.328

B. Write your answers in the blanks provided.

✓ In 25.639, what is the place value of the digit 3? **hundredths**

✓ In 8.146.7, what is the place value of the digit 7? **tenths**

✓ In 112.58, which digit is in the hundredths place? **8**

✓ In 40.245, which digit is in the tenths place? **2**

✓ What number is 10 times larger than 0.526? **5.26**

Lesson 72

Dividing Decimals

A. Find the quotient for each division problem.

$$3\overline{)90.6} = 30.2 \qquad 7\overline{)44.8} = 6.4 \qquad 4\overline{)1.56} = 0.39 \qquad 6\overline{)9.48} = 1.58$$

B. Solve each word problem. Use the space on the right for your work area.

Kyle bought 5 pounds of candies and paid a total of $32.50. What is the price per pound?

$6.50

Orson drew a hexagon with a perimeter of 14.4 inches. How long is each side of the hexagon?

2.4 inches

During the weekend, Jenny drove 85.2 miles. She used 3 gallons of gas. How many miles did she drive per gallon of gas?

28.4 miles

Lesson 73

Fractions and Decimals

A. Convert between fractions and decimals.

$$0.1 = \frac{1}{10} \qquad 0.24 = \frac{24}{100} \qquad 0.493 = \frac{493}{1000}$$

$$\frac{3}{10} = 0.3 \qquad \frac{47}{100} = 0.47 \qquad \frac{705}{1000} = 0.705$$

B. Convert the fractions to decimals. To convert a fraction to a decimal:

First, write the fraction as a division problem.
Second, add a decimal point and zeros to the dividend.
Third, divide and place a decimal point in the quotient.

$$\frac{1}{2} = 0.5 \qquad \frac{3}{4} = 0.75 \qquad \frac{5}{8} = 0.625$$

$$\frac{1}{5} = 0.2 \qquad \frac{9}{20} = 0.45 \qquad \frac{7}{25} = 0.28$$

YOUR WORK AREA

The first one:
$$\begin{array}{r} 0.5 \\ 2\overline{)1.000} \\ \underline{1\ 0} \\ 0 \end{array}$$

Lesson 74

Fractions and Decimals

Draw lines to match the fractions and decimals.

$^{11}/_{25}$ • • 0.15 $0.\overline{6}$ • • $^1/_8$

$^9/_{10}$ • • 0.44 0.750 • • $^2/_3$

$^3/_{20}$ • • 0.34 0.125 • • $^1/_9$

$^{17}/_{50}$ • • 0.84 0.375 • • $^3/_8$

$^{21}/_{25}$ • • 0.90 $0.\overline{1}$ • • $^3/_4$

YOUR WORK AREA

Lesson 75

Fractions and Decimals & Adding Fractions

A. Draw lines to match the fractions and decimals.

1 3/4 • • 0.125   3.000 • • 3

1/8 • • 5.000   3.250 • • 2 5/8

5 • • 1.750   2.625 • • 2 3/4

1 1/2 • • 1.500   2.750 • • 3/8

1/4 • • 0.250   0.375 • • 3 1/4

B. Add and subtract the fractions. Simplify your answers as much as possible.

$$\frac{4}{9} + \frac{2}{9} = \frac{6}{9} = \frac{2}{3} \qquad \frac{3}{4} - \frac{1}{4} = \frac{2}{4} = \frac{1}{2}$$

$$\frac{2}{6} + \frac{1}{6} = \frac{3}{6} = \frac{1}{2} \qquad \frac{5}{8} - \frac{3}{8} = \frac{2}{8} = \frac{1}{4}$$

YOUR WORK AREA

Lesson 76

Adding Decimals

Add the decimals. To add decimals:

First, write the decimals vertically with the decimal points lined up.
Second, pad with zeros so the numbers have the same length.
Third, add the numbers as you would add whole numbers.
Fourth, carry the decimal point directly down into your answer.

$$1.3 + 1.45 = 2.75 \qquad 0.6 + 1.257 = 1.857$$

$$5 + 2.308 = 7.308 \qquad 3.25 + 0.075 = 3.325$$

$$2.0 + 0.2 + 0.02 + 0.002 = 2.222$$

$$101 + 10.1 + 1.01 + 0.101 = 112.211$$

$$502.03 + 78.3054 + 40.039 + 1.1326 = 621.507$$

YOUR WORK AREA

The first one:
$$\begin{array}{r} 1.30 \\ + \ 1.45 \\ \hline 1.75 \end{array}$$

Lesson 77

Subtracting Decimals

Subtract the decimals. To subtract decimals:

First, write the decimals vertically with the decimal points lined up.
Second, pad with zeros so the numbers have the same length.
Third, subtract the numbers as you would subtract whole numbers.
Fourth, carry the decimal point directly down into your answer.

$$1.1 - 0.03 = 1.07 \qquad 7.205 - 0.55 = 6.655$$

$$2.9 - 1.02 = 1.88 \qquad 17.094 - 4.23 = 12.864$$

$$8 - 0.402 = 7.598 \qquad 20.023 - 3.05 = 16.973$$

$$3 - 2.061 = 0.939 \qquad 103.8 - 4.902 = 98.898$$

YOUR WORK AREA

The first one:
$$\begin{array}{r} 1.10 \\ - \ 0.03 \\ \hline 1.07 \end{array}$$

Lesson 78

Multiplying Decimals

Multiply the decimals. To multiply decimals:

First, ignore the decimal points and multiply as usual.
Second, count the total number of decimal places in the factors.
Third, place a decimal point in your answer so that
your answer has the same number of decimal places as you counted.

$0.03 \times 1.1 =$ __0.033__ $\qquad$ $0.091 \times 0.2 =$ __0.0182__

$0.25 \times 0.2 =$ __0.05__ $\qquad$ $0.007 \times 1.6 =$ __0.0112__

$0.04 \times 1.4 =$ __0.056__ $\qquad$ $0.213 \times 0.5 =$ __0.1065__

$0.05 \times 2.8 =$ __0.14__ $\qquad$ $0.428 \times 0.3 =$ __0.1284__

YOUR WORK AREA
The first one!

```
   0.03
 x  1.1
 ------
  0.033
```

Lesson 79

Multiplying Decimals

A. Solve the multiplication problems.

0.2	0.6	0.5	0.4
x 0.8	x 0.4	x 0.9	x 0.2
0.16	0.24	0.45	0.08
0.05	0.68	0.435	0.957
x 3.7	x 2.4	x 4.6	x 0.8
0.185	1.632	2.001	0.7656

B. Can you solve this riddle? Use the clues to find the 7-digit number.

9	,	3	2	9	.	3	5	2

Divide 79 by 7. Write the remainder in the tens and thousandths places.

Add the number in the tens place to the number of days in a week. Write the answer in the thousands and ones places.

Multiply the number in the tens place by the number in the ones place and then divide the result by 5. Write the remainder in the hundreds and tenths places.

Add 3 to the number in the tens places. Write the result in the hundredths place.

Lesson 80

Multiplying Decimals

Solve the multiplication problems.

0.86	0.96	0.54	0.88
x 0.48	x 0.59	x 0.43	x 0.93
0.4128	0.5664	0.2322	0.8184
0.67	0.75	0.62	0.84
x 0.54	x 0.45	x 0.12	x 0.97
0.3618	0.3375	0.0744	0.8148
0.61	0.19	0.11	0.31
x 0.95	x 0.72	x 0.33	x 0.84
0.5795	0.1368	0.0363	0.2604

Lesson 81

Adding and Subtracting Decimals

A. Solve the addition and subtraction problems.

4.2	3.9	4.8	1.4	7.8
+ 2.7	+ 6.5	+ 5.9	+ 5.8	+ 5.6
6.9	10.4	10.7	7.2	13.4
6.8	7.9	8.5	9.7	11.9
− 2.4	− 4.2	− 3.5	− 9.2	− 0.4
4.4	3.7	5.0	0.5	11.5
7.2	3.4	15.3	13.5	14.2
− 5.9	− 2.8	− 8.5	− 5.9	− 8.6
1.3	0.6	6.8	7.6	5.6

B. Can you solve these square puzzles? For each puzzle, arrange the numbers 1 to 9 in the grid so that each row, column, and diagonal adds up to 15.

2	7	6
9	5	1
4	3	8

4	9	2
3	5	7
8	1	6

Lesson 82

Making Change

Determine how much change you would receive. Find the fewest number of coins possible to show the change you receive. The first one is done for you!

You buy	You pay	You receive	25¢	10¢	5¢	1¢
$57.63	$60.00	$2.37	9	1	0	2
$32.45	$50.00	$17.55	70	0	1	0
$40.29	$50.00	$9.71	38	2	0	1
$55.87	$60.00	$4.13	16	1	0	3
$21.02	$30.00	$8.98	35	2	0	3
$64.36	$80.00	$15.64	62	1	0	4
$20.99	$40.00	$19.01	76	0	0	1
$75.30	$80.00	$4.70	18	2	0	0
$17.05	$20.00	$2.95	11	2	0	0
$46.24	$50.00	$3.76	15	0	0	1

Lesson 83

Making Change

Determine how much change you would receive. Find the fewest number of coins possible to show the change you receive.

You buy	You pay	You receive	25¢	10¢	5¢	1¢
$0.73	$1.00	$0.27	1	0	0	2
$0.99	$1.00	$0.01	0	0	0	1
$0.27	$1.00	$0.73	2	2	0	3
$0.55	$1.00	$0.45	1	2	0	0
$3.42	$10.00	$6.58	26	0	1	3
$7.90	$10.00	$2.10	8	1	0	0

$100.00	$100.00	$100.00
− $47.52	− $90.16	− $50.01
$52.48	$9.84	$49.99

Lesson 84

Dividing Decimals

Divide the decimals. To divide decimals:

First, move the decimal points in the divisor and dividend to the right to make the divisor a whole number.
Second, ignore the decimal points and divide as usual.
Third, place a decimal point in the quotient directly above the decimal point in the dividend.

$0.91 \div 0.7 =$ __1.3__ $\qquad$ $9.84 \div 8 =$ __1.23__

$6.4 \div 0.4 =$ __16__ $\qquad$ $16.52 \div 7 =$ __2.36__

$14.4 \div 1.2 =$ __12__ $\qquad$ $0.275 \div 0.05 =$ __5.5__

$5.39 \div 1.1 =$ __4.9__ $\qquad$ $2.405 \div 0.37 =$ __6.5__

YOUR WORK AREA
The first one!

```
      1.3
  7 ) 9.1
      7
      ---
      2 1
      2 1
      ---
        0
```

Lesson 85

Three Division Formats

Write each division problem in three different formats.

using a division symbol	using a long division symbol	as a fraction
$12 \div 3$ =	$3\overline{)12}$ =	$12/3$
$57 \div 6$ =	$6\overline{)57}$ =	$57/6$
$17 \div 12$ =	$12\overline{)17}$ =	$17/12$
$48 \div 25$ =	$25\overline{)48}$ =	$48/25$
$35 \div 35$ =	$35\overline{)35}$ =	$35/35$
$50 \div 18$ =	$18\overline{)50}$ =	$50/18$
$81 \div 95$ =	$95\overline{)81}$ =	$81/95$
$72 \div 60$ =	$60\overline{)72}$ =	$72/60$
$57 \div 4$ =	$4\overline{)57}$ =	$57/4$
$63 \div 17$ =	$17\overline{)63}$ =	$63/17$

Lesson 86

Comparing Fractions and Decimals

Compare the fractions and decimals using < or >. Convert each fraction to a decimal by dividing the numerator by the denominator and then compare the decimals. (Hint: Stop dividing once you find out which number is bigger.)

0.4 $(<)$ $\frac{1}{2} = 0.5$ $\qquad$ 0.814 $(>)$ $\frac{5}{7} = 0.71...$

0.85 $(>)$ $\frac{3}{4} = 0.75$ $\qquad$ 0.606 $(<)$ $\frac{2}{3} = 0.66...$

0.5 $(>)$ $\frac{2}{5} = 0.4$ $\qquad$ 0.042 $(<)$ $\frac{1}{7} = 0.14...$

0.75 $(<)$ $\frac{7}{8} = 0.875$ $\qquad$ 0.625 $(>)$ $\frac{5}{9} = 0.55...$

0.45 $(>)$ $\frac{1}{4} = 0.25$ $\qquad$ 0.222 $(<)$ $\frac{1}{3} = 0.33...$

YOUR WORK AREA

Lesson 87

Multiplying 3-Digits
Complete five problems. For every incorrect answer, do an extra problem.

503	652	569	706
x 213	x 520	x 498	x 568
107,139	339,040	283,362	401,008

744	187	381	943
x 105	x 436	x 255	x 625
78,120	81,532	97,155	589,375

Lesson 88

Dividing by 2-Digits
Complete five problems. For every incorrect answer, do an extra problem.

$$72\overline{)2926} \quad 19\overline{)6292} \quad 55\overline{)4419} \quad 34\overline{)8013}$$

A = 40 R 46   C = 80 R 19

B = 331 R 3   D = 235 R 23

$$48\overline{)7593} \quad 23\overline{)4328} \quad 89\overline{)2244} \quad 41\overline{)5310}$$

E = 158 R 9   G = 25 R 19

F = 188 R 4   H = 129 R 21

Lesson 89

Adding Fractions
Add the fractions. Simplify your answers as much as possible.

$\frac{1}{3} + \frac{1}{3} = \frac{2}{3}$ $\frac{3}{9} + \frac{2}{9} = \frac{5}{9}$

$\frac{2}{8} + \frac{4}{8} = \frac{6}{8} = \frac{3}{4}$ $\frac{2}{5} + \frac{1}{5} = \frac{3}{5}$

$\frac{1}{6} + \frac{3}{6} = \frac{4}{6} = \frac{2}{3}$ $\frac{1}{4} + \frac{1}{4} = \frac{2}{4} = \frac{1}{2}$

$\frac{2}{9} + \frac{4}{9} = \frac{6}{9} = \frac{2}{3}$ $\frac{3}{8} + \frac{1}{8} = \frac{4}{8} = \frac{1}{2}$

$\frac{2}{5} + \frac{2}{5} = \frac{4}{5}$ $\frac{4}{7} + \frac{2}{7} = \frac{6}{7}$

$\frac{1}{7} + \frac{3}{7} = \frac{4}{7}$ $\frac{2}{9} + \frac{1}{9} = \frac{3}{9} = \frac{1}{3}$

$\frac{2}{4} + \frac{1}{4} = \frac{3}{4}$ $\frac{4}{8} + \frac{3}{8} = \frac{7}{8}$

$\frac{3}{9} + \frac{3}{9} = \frac{6}{9} = \frac{2}{3}$ $\frac{1}{6} + \frac{2}{6} = \frac{3}{6} = \frac{1}{2}$

Lesson 90

Fractions and Decimals & Adding Fractions
A. Draw lines to match the fractions and decimals.

1/2 • • 0.6̄   0.25 • • 4/6
3/4 • • 0.5   0.6̄ • • 1/3
2/3 • • 0.25   0.5 • • 2/8
1/4 • • 0.75   0.3̄ • • 2/4

B. Write the addition sentence that represents each picture, and solve it.

$1\frac{5}{6} + 2\frac{4}{6} = 4\frac{3}{6} = 4\frac{1}{2}$

$2\frac{1}{3} + 1\frac{2}{3} = 3\frac{3}{3} = 4$

$3\frac{3}{4} + 2\frac{1}{4} = 5\frac{4}{4} = 6$

$2\frac{3}{6} + 2\frac{5}{6} = 5\frac{2}{6} = 5\frac{1}{3}$

Lesson 91

Multiplying Fractions
A. Multiply the fractions. To multiply fractions:

First, multiply the top numbers (the numerators).
Second, multiply the bottom numbers (the denominators).
Third, simplify (or reduce) the fraction if needed.

$\frac{1}{2} \times \frac{2}{5} = \frac{2}{10} = \frac{1}{5}$ $\frac{5}{8} \times \frac{7}{10} = \frac{35}{80} = \frac{7}{16}$

$\frac{3}{4} \times \frac{5}{6} = \frac{15}{24} = \frac{5}{8}$ $\frac{7}{3} \times \frac{5}{14} = \frac{35}{42} = \frac{5}{6}$

$\frac{2}{7} \times \frac{4}{3} = \frac{8}{21}$ $\frac{3}{10} \times 5 = \frac{15}{10} = \frac{3}{2} = 1\frac{1}{2}$

$\frac{5}{6} \times \frac{2}{9} = \frac{10}{54} = \frac{5}{27}$ $\frac{5}{12} \times 6 = \frac{30}{12} = \frac{5}{2} = 2\frac{1}{2}$

$\frac{3}{4} \times \frac{2}{5} \times \frac{5}{8} = \frac{30}{160} = \frac{3}{16}$

$\frac{5}{8} \times \frac{3}{12} \times \frac{7}{10} = \frac{105}{960} = \frac{7}{64}$

B. Complete the next worksheet, too.

Lesson 91

Timed Addition
B. Time yourself to see how fast you can solve all the problems.

7 + 8 = 15	3 + 4 = 7	9 + 1 = 10
5 + 2 = 7	3 + 7 = 10	8 + 7 = 15
4 + 4 = 8	3 + 5 = 8	2 + 9 = 11
6 + 7 = 13	5 + 5 = 10	2 + 2 = 4
9 + 3 = 12	4 + 2 = 6	4 + 6 = 10
5 + 8 = 13	8 + 6 = 14	8 + 3 = 11
7 + 7 = 14	9 + 2 = 11	5 + 9 = 14
2 + 3 = 5	6 + 5 = 11	7 + 5 = 12
6 + 8 = 16	8 + 8 = 16	6 + 2 = 8
9 + 7 = 16	5 + 6 = 11	9 + 6 = 15
8 + 5 = 13	2 + 4 = 6	3 + 8 = 11
2 + 8 = 10	3 + 6 = 9	9 + 9 = 18
6 + 3 = 9	6 + 9 = 15	2 + 7 = 9
9 + 5 = 14	3 + 9 = 12	4 + 8 = 12
7 + 3 = 10	4 + 7 = 11	3 + 2 = 5
8 + 4 = 12	4 + 9 = 13	7 + 9 = 16
3 + 3 = 6	8 + 2 = 10	2 + 6 = 8
6 + 4 = 10	4 + 5 = 9	5 + 7 = 12
7 + 6 = 13	2 + 5 = 7	9 + 4 = 13
9 + 8 = 17	6 + 6 = 12	Time: _____

Lesson 92

Dividing by 1-Digit & Multiplying Fractions
A. Find the quotient and remainder for each division problem.

$$8\overline{)236} = 29\,R\,4 \quad 7\overline{)150} = 21\,R\,3 \quad 9\overline{)769} = 85\,R\,4 \quad 2\overline{)125} = 62\,R\,1$$

B. Multiply the fractions. Simplify your answers as much as possible.

$\frac{1}{2} \times \frac{4}{7} = \frac{4}{14} = \frac{2}{7}$ $\frac{2}{11} \times \frac{1}{6} = \frac{2}{66} = \frac{1}{33}$

$\frac{3}{4} \times \frac{2}{9} = \frac{6}{36} = \frac{1}{6}$ $\frac{9}{10} \times \frac{1}{3} = \frac{9}{30} = \frac{3}{10}$

$\frac{2}{7} \times \frac{4}{6} = \frac{8}{42} = \frac{4}{21}$ $\frac{7}{12} \times \frac{3}{4} = \frac{21}{48} = \frac{7}{16}$

$\frac{3}{8} \times \frac{2}{5} = \frac{6}{40} = \frac{3}{20}$ $\frac{6}{15} \times \frac{5}{9} = \frac{30}{135} = \frac{2}{9}$

C. Complete the next worksheet, too.

Lesson 92

Timed Multiplication
C. Time yourself to see how fast you can solve all the problems.

3 x 7 = 21	3 x 4 = 12	9 x 4 = 36
5 x 2 = 10	5 x 6 = 30	8 x 7 = 56
4 x 4 = 16	3 x 5 = 15	2 x 9 = 18
6 x 7 = 42	5 x 5 = 25	5 x 4 = 20
9 x 3 = 27	4 x 3 = 12	4 x 6 = 24
5 x 8 = 40	8 x 6 = 48	8 x 3 = 24
8 x 4 = 32	9 x 2 = 18	2 x 6 = 12
7 x 2 = 14	6 x 5 = 30	7 x 5 = 35
6 x 8 = 48	4 x 7 = 28	6 x 2 = 12
9 x 7 = 63	8 x 5 = 40	9 x 6 = 54
1 x 6 = 6	2 x 4 = 8	4 x 8 = 32
2 x 8 = 16	3 x 6 = 18	9 x 9 = 81
6 x 3 = 18	6 x 9 = 54	2 x 7 = 14
9 x 5 = 45	3 x 9 = 27	7 x 4 = 28
7 x 3 = 21	8 x 8 = 64	8 x 9 = 72
5 x 9 = 45	4 x 9 = 36	7 x 9 = 63
3 x 3 = 9	8 x 2 = 16	7 x 7 = 49
6 x 4 = 24	4 x 5 = 20	5 x 7 = 35
7 x 6 = 42	2 x 5 = 10	3 x 8 = 24
9 x 8 = 72	6 x 6 = 36	Time: _____

Lesson 93

Dividing Fractions
A. Divide the fractions. To divide fractions:

First, flip the second fraction upside down to make a reciprocal.
Second, multiply the first fraction by the reciprocal.
Third, simplify (or reduce) the fraction if needed.

$\frac{2}{3} \div \frac{1}{4} = \frac{8}{3} = 2\frac{2}{3}$ $\frac{1}{12} \div \frac{1}{4} = \frac{4}{12} = \frac{1}{3}$

$\frac{1}{2} \div \frac{1}{6} = \frac{6}{2} = 3$ $\frac{7}{18} \div \frac{2}{3} = \frac{21}{36} = \frac{7}{12}$

$\frac{6}{8} \div \frac{3}{4} = \frac{24}{24} = 1$ $\frac{15}{4} \div \frac{3}{8} = \frac{120}{12} = 10$

$\frac{3}{4} \div \frac{5}{6} = \frac{18}{20} = \frac{9}{10}$ $\frac{7}{5} \div \frac{9}{10} = \frac{70}{45} = \frac{14}{9} = 1\frac{5}{9}$

$\frac{3}{7} \div \frac{6}{7} = \frac{21}{42} = \frac{1}{2}$ $\frac{7}{8} \div \frac{5}{16} = \frac{112}{40} = \frac{14}{5} = 2\frac{4}{5}$

B. Complete the next worksheet, too.

Lesson 93

Timed Subtraction

B. Time yourself to see how fast you can solve all the problems.

14 – 7 = 7	13 – 8 = 5	16 – 7 = 9
12 – 6 = 6	15 – 7 = 8	11 – 3 = 8
17 – 9 = 8	10 – 4 = 6	5 – 3 = 2
11 – 4 = 7	14 – 5 = 9	13 – 4 = 9
13 – 5 = 8	9 – 2 = 7	8 – 6 = 2
6 – 3 = 3	10 – 9 = 1	12 – 7 = 5
15 – 6 = 9	8 – 5 = 3	18 – 9 = 9
12 – 9 = 3	12 – 3 = 9	10 – 3 = 7
9 – 3 = 6	7 – 4 = 3	9 – 7 = 2
14 – 9 = 5	11 – 2 = 9	15 – 8 = 7
8 – 4 = 4	17 – 8 = 9	12 – 4 = 8
11 – 8 = 3	10 – 2 = 8	13 – 6 = 7
15 – 9 = 6	13 – 7 = 6	11 – 5 = 6
9 – 4 = 5	8 – 3 = 5	14 – 6 = 8
12 – 5 = 7	9 – 6 = 3	5 – 2 = 3
16 – 9 = 7	11 – 7 = 4	16 – 8 = 8
7 – 5 = 2	10 – 5 = 5	10 – 7 = 3
11 – 6 = 5	12 – 8 = 4	9 – 5 = 4
10 – 8 = 2	14 – 8 = 6	11 – 9 = 2
13 – 9 =	10 – 6 = 4	Time: _____

Lesson 94

Dividing by 1-Digit

A. Find the quotient and remainder for each division problem.

$$8\overline{)307} = 38\,R\,3 \qquad 3\overline{)975} = 325 \qquad 4\overline{)898} = 224\,R\,2 \qquad 7\overline{)566} = 80\,R\,6$$

$$5\overline{)743} = 148\,R\,3 \qquad 6\overline{)910} = 151\,R\,4 \qquad 5\overline{)132} = 26\,R\,2 \qquad 2\overline{)809} = 404\,R\,1$$

B. Complete the next worksheet, too.

Lesson 94

Timed Division

B. Find the quotient, and write the remainder as a fraction. Time yourself, too!

15 ÷ 5 = 3	47 ÷ 9 = 5 2/9	35 ÷ 5 = 7
45 ÷ 7 = 6 3/7	12 ÷ 3 = 4	22 ÷ 9 = 2 4/9
24 ÷ 3 = 8	47 ÷ 6 = 7 5/6	72 ÷ 8 = 9
37 ÷ 4 = 9 1/4	56 ÷ 9 = 6 2/9	37 ÷ 6 = 6 1/6
16 ÷ 8 = 2	21 ÷ 3 = 7	56 ÷ 7 = 8
36 ÷ 9 = 4	19 ÷ 2 = 9 1/2	81 ÷ 9 = 9
37 ÷ 7 = 5 2/7	40 ÷ 5 = 8	68 ÷ 7 = 9 5/7
29 ÷ 4 = 7 1/4	49 ÷ 7 = 7	18 ÷ 6 = 3
55 ÷ 6 = 9 1/6	53 ÷ 6 = 8 5/6	59 ÷ 8 = 7 3/8
23 ÷ 4 = 5 3/4	9 ÷ 1 = 9	35 ÷ 4 = 8 3/4
12 ÷ 6 = 2	20 ÷ 5 = 4	40 ÷ 8 = 5
20 ÷ 3 = 6 2/3	16 ÷ 2 = 8	11 ÷ 4 = 2 3/4
69 ÷ 8 = 8 5/8	15 ÷ 4 = 3 3/4	35 ÷ 6 = 5 5/6
27 ÷ 4 = 6 3/4	25 ÷ 6 = 4 1/6	29 ÷ 9 = 3 2/9
30 ÷ 3 = 10	25 ÷ 5 = 5	17 ÷ 3 = 5 2/3
35 ÷ 8 = 4 3/8	67 ÷ 9 = 7 4/9	51 ÷ 8 = 6 3/8
26 ÷ 7 = 3 5/7	24 ÷ 8 = 3	14 ÷ 7 = 2
72 ÷ 9 = 8	28 ÷ 7 = 4	19 ÷ 4 = 4 3/4
3 ÷ 2 = 1 1/2	48 ÷ 5 = 9 3/5	30 ÷ 5 = 6
12 ÷ 5 = 2 2/5	12 ÷ 2 = 6	Time: _____

Lesson 95

Dividing Fractions

A. Divide the fractions and whole numbers. Simplify your answers if possible.

$$2 \div \frac{1}{2} = 4 \qquad\qquad \frac{9}{10} \div 3 = \frac{9}{30} = \frac{3}{10}$$

$$\frac{2}{3} \div 8 = \frac{2}{24} = \frac{1}{12} \qquad 16 \div \frac{8}{9} = \frac{144}{8} = 18$$

$$\frac{1}{2} \div 7 = \frac{1}{14} \qquad\qquad 8 \div \frac{4}{10} = \frac{80}{4} = 20$$

$$9 \div \frac{1}{3} = 27 \qquad\qquad \frac{3}{5} \div 12 = \frac{3}{60} = \frac{1}{20}$$

$$\frac{3}{5} \div 9 = \frac{3}{45} = \frac{1}{15} \qquad 5 \div \frac{7}{10} = \frac{50}{7} = 7\frac{1}{7}$$

B. Can you solve this riddle? Use the clues to find the correct fraction.

$\frac{7}{8}$	$\frac{2}{6}$	$\frac{6}{4}$
$\frac{3}{12}$	$\frac{4}{8}$	$\frac{4}{9}$

I am a proper fraction.
My value is bigger than a third.
I am not equivalent to 1/2.
My numerator is even.
What am I? Circle me!

Lesson 96

Mean, Median, Mode, and Range

Find the mean, median, mode, and range in each set of values. To calculate the mean, median, mode, and range:

- Mean = the sum of all values / the number of values
- Median = the middle value when values are sorted
- Mode = the value which appears most frequently
- Range = the highest value – the lowest value

Values	Mean	Median	Mode	Range
3, 6, 5, 3, 3	4	3	3	3
5, 8, 4, 3, 4, 7, 4	5	4	4	5
16, 23, 18, 23, 20	20	20	23	7
4.5, 6.7, 3.9, 4.5, 4.9	4.9	4.5	4.5	2.8

YOUR WORK AREA

Lesson 97

Mean, Median, Mode, and Range

Solve each word problem. Use the space on the right for your work area.

Find the range of Sam's math scores:
89, 73, 84, 91, 77, 94

21

Find the mean of these numbers:
1.5, 0.2, 2.7, 0.6, 0.3, 1.9

1.2

Find the median of these numbers:
2.4, 2.5, 2.9, 2.7, 2.9, 2.0, 2.1

2.5

Find the mode of these numbers:
65, 68, 61, 68, 45, 65, 65, 53

65

Find the mean cost of Sam's textbooks:
$8, $8, $9, $16, $16, $16, $18

$13

The mean of three numbers is 9. Two of the numbers are 12 and 8. What is the third number?

7

Lesson 98

Mean, Median, and Mode & Dividing Fractions

A. Find the mean, median, and mode of the following data set.

80, 84, 78, 11, 90, 51, 84, 14, 14, 84, 48

YOUR WORK AREA

Mean: **58**   Median: **78**   Mode: **84**

B. Divide the fractions.

$$\frac{2}{5} \div \frac{3}{4} = \frac{8}{15} \qquad \frac{7}{10} \div \frac{2}{5} = \frac{35}{20} = \frac{7}{4} = 1\frac{3}{4}$$

$$\frac{1}{6} \div \frac{5}{9} = \frac{9}{30} = \frac{3}{10} \qquad 15 \div \frac{3}{7} = \frac{105}{3} = 35$$

$$8 \div \frac{1}{4} = 32 \qquad \frac{7}{8} \div \frac{5}{12} = \frac{84}{40} = \frac{21}{10} = 2\frac{1}{10}$$

$$\frac{4}{9} \div 6 = \frac{4}{54} = \frac{2}{27} \qquad \frac{6}{7} \div 18 = \frac{6}{126} = \frac{1}{21}$$

Lesson 99

Mean, Median, Mode, and Range

A. Find the mean, median, mode, and range in each set of values.

Values	Mean	Median	Mode	Range
6, 6, 7, 6, 5	6	6	6	2
9, 2, 7, 5, 7, 7, 5	6	7	7	7
8, 5, 9, 6, 8, 8, 5, 5, 9	7	8	5, 8	4
7, 6, 6, 7, 9, 7, 7, 6, 8	7	7	7	3

YOUR WORK AREA

B. Solve each word problem. Use the space on the right for your work area.

The mean of five numbers is 6. The four numbers are 3, 4, 6, and 8. What is the fifth number?

9

The mean of four numbers is 6. The mode is 5 and it occurs three times. Find the four numbers.

5, 5, 5, 9

Find the mean of the first five multiples of 2 (the first five even numbers).

6

Lesson 100

Making Change & Rounding Numbers

A. Determine how much change you would receive. Find the fewest number of coins possible to show the change you receive.

You buy	You pay	You receive	25¢	10¢	5¢	1¢
			Coins you receive			
$33.53	$35.00	$1.47	5	2	0	2
$40.60	$45.00	$4.40	17	1	1	0
$25.87	$40.00	$14.13	56	1	0	3
$30.24	$35.00	$4.76	19	0	0	1
$65.52	$70.00	$4.48	17	2	0	3
$48.07	$50.00	$1.93	7	1	1	3

B. Round each number to the nearest ten, hundred, and thousand.

	3,877	7,478	9,694	34,162
Nearest 10	3,880	7,480	9,690	34,160
Nearest 100	3,900	7,500	9,700	34,200
Nearest 1000	4,000	7,000	10,000	34,000

Lesson 101

Percentages

A. Percent means "per 100" or "out of 100" and we use the symbol "%" to represent it. Write the percent of the shaded portion in each grid.

5 % 　　　 50 % 　　　 100 %

B. Calculate the percentage of each quantity. The first one is done for you!

10 out of 100	65 out of 100	140 out of 200
10%	65%	70%

15 out of 50	12 out of 25	9 out of 10
30%	48%	90%

C. Calculate the value of each percent. The first one is done for you!

15% of 100	80% of 100	50% of 200
15	80	100

25% out of 80	20% of 50	60% of 10
20	10	6

Lesson 102

Fractions, Decimals, and Percentages

A. Convert between decimals and percents.

0.01 =	1%	75% =	0.75
0.25 =	25%	3.5% =	0.035
0.875 =	87.5%	12.5% =	0.125
3.025 =	302.5%	18.75% =	0.1875

B. Convert the fractions to decimals and percents. YOUR WORK AREA

$1/4$ = 0.25 = 25%

$3/5$ = 0.6 = 60%

$11/20$ = 0.55 = 55%

C. Convert the decimals to percents and fractions.

0.5 = 50% = $50/100$ = $1/2$

0.8 = 80% = $80/100$ = $4/5$

0.75 = 75% = $75/100$ = $3/4$

Lesson 103

Fractions, Decimals, and Percentages

A. Convert the decimals to percents.

0.7 =	70%	0.007 =	0.7%
0.3 =	30%	0.571 =	57.1%
0.32 =	32%	0.019 =	1.9%
2.05 =	205%	4.125 =	412.5%
1.86 =	186%	8.604 =	860.4%

B. Convert the fractions to decimals and percents. YOUR WORK AREA

$7/10$ = 0.7 = 70%

$1/2$ = 0.5 = 50%

$5/4$ = 1.25 = 125%

$8/5$ = 1.6 = 160%

$3/20$ = 0.15 = 15%

$9/25$ = 0.36 = 36%

Lesson 104

Fractions, Decimals, and Percentages

Fractions, decimals, and percents are different ways of showing the same value. Complete the table below. Simplify the fractions as much as possible.

Fraction	Decimal	Percent	YOUR WORK AREA
$9/25$	0.36	36%	
$1/4$	0.25	25%	
$1/8$	0.125	12.5%	
$3/5$	0.6	60%	
$7/20$	0.35	35%	
$2/10$	0.2	20%	
$3/8$	0.375	37.5%	
$1/2$	0.5	50%	
$4/5$	0.8	80%	
$3/4$	0.75	75%	

Lesson 105

Fractions and Decimals & Decimal Place Value

A. Convert the decimals to percents and fractions.

0.1 = 10% = $1/10$　　YOUR WORK AREA

1.8 = 180% = $9/5$

1.25 = 125% = $5/4$

B. Convert the fractions to decimals and percents.

$4\frac{1}{2}$ = 4.5 = 450%

$7\frac{3}{4}$ = 7.75 = 775%

$3\frac{2}{25}$ = 3.08 = 308%

C. Write each number in standard form.

✓ 3 tens + 4 ones + 7 tenths + 2 thousandths = 　34.702

✓ 8 hundreds + 6 tens + 5 tenths + 1 hundredth = 　860.51

✓ 2 tens + 7 ones + 2 hundredths + 4 thousandths = 　27.024

✓ 1 one + 5 thousands + 9 hundredths + 3 tenths = 　5,001.39

✓ 5 thousands + 8 tenths + 3 tens + 6 hundredths = 　5,030.86

Lesson 106

Word Problems

Solve each word problem. Use the space on the right for your work area.

A TV originally cost $500. If the price of the TV increases by 10%, what is the new price?

$550

$5.00 candy bars are now on sale for 20% off. What will the candy bars cost now?

$4.00

The dinner bill was $30 and Mr. Kim left a 25% tip. How much did Mr. Kim pay for the dinner?

$37.50

Jack's new laptop was $850 plus the 8% tax. How much did Jack pay for his laptop?

$918

The population of Mia's city was 200,000 last year. This year the population grew by 5%. What is the population of Mia's city this year?

210,000

The gym membership fee is $60 per month. If Heather signs up for one whole year, she'll receive 20% off the total annual cost. What will be her actual cost for one year?

$576

Lesson 107

Story Problems

Read the stories and find the answers.

Rebekah recycles 15 cans each month. How many cans does she recycle in a year?	180
Bristol's songbird sings 3 songs every day. How many songs will the songbird sing in 4 weeks?	84
Daniel's worksheet had 15 questions. Daniel got 12 correct. How many questions did he get wrong?	3
The robotics team has 5 members. Sarah quit and Brooke joined the group. Then Braden joined the group and Sarah rejoined the group, how many members are now in the robotics team?	7
Jessica had $70 from her birthday. She bought a shirt for $15 and a skirt for $25. Then she bought accessories that cost $20. How much did she spend and how much money does she have left?	$60, $10
Kaitlyn ate 1/4 of a pizza. Nathaniel ate 3/4 of a pizza. Then they had cake. Kaitlyn ate 4/5 and Nathaniel ate 1/5 of the cake. How much pizza and cake did they eat?	1 each
Our homeschool group included 11 high school students, 35 middle school students, 23 elementary students, 31 parents, and 17 kids in the nursery. How many people were in our group in all?	117
Michael told Ezra he could share his candies, but Michael didn't know how much they should each get. Ezra was so smart, he told Michael they should each get 50%. How many did they each get if there were 34 candies?	17

YOUR WORK AREA

Lesson 108

Word Problems

Solve each word problem. Use the space on the right for your work area.

Kyle can solve 6 division problems in one minute. How many problems can Kyle solve in 8 minutes?

48 problems

A recipe calls for 9 apples to make one apple pie. Kate has 63 apples. How many pies can she make?

7 pies

Dana is reading a novel. She read 15 pages each day for 8 days, and she still has 28 pages left. How many pages are in Dana's book?

148 pages

Leah has 5 stickers. Kate has 3 times as many stickers as Leah. Matt has 4 times as many stickers as Kate. How many stickers does Matt have?

60 stickers

Stacy has 98 cents. She wants to buy 6 candy bars. Each candy bar costs 12 cents. How much money will Stacy have left?

26 cents

Ron is preparing for his vocabulary test. If he learns 12 new words each day, how many days will it take Ron to learn all 144 words on his list?

12 days

Lesson 109

Word Problems

Solve each word problem. Use the space on the right for your work area.

The auditorium has 95 seats. 47 people sat down to listen to a lecture. 30 people were outside talking to each other. How many seats were empty?

48 seats

Laura invited 52 people to her party. She bought 35 sandwiches. 15 people can't come to the party. How many people will be at Laura's party?

37 people

The grocery store had 72 bags of potatoes. Each bag weighs 5 pounds. The store sold 56 bags. How many bags of potatoes does the store have left?

16 bags

Max has 28 marbles. Jim has 9 fewer marbles than Max. Sam has 16 more marbles than Max. How many marbles does Sam have?

44 marbles

Ron had 90 cents. He bought a cookie for 25 cents and a candy bar for 38 cents. How much money did Ron spend in all?

63 cents

Lucy is going on a 33 mile hike. Her backpack weighs 18 pounds. She hiked 16 miles on the first day. How many miles does Lucy have left?

17 miles

Lesson 110

Word Problems

Our homeschool group is planning a picnic. Eighty people are expected to come. Read the questions and find the answers.

Dylan is baking cookies for the picnic. He wants to prepare 3 cookies per person. A recipe calls for 1 egg to make a dozen cookies. Eggs are sold in cartons of 12. How many cartons of eggs should Dylan buy?

2 cartons

Rebekah decided to bake peach pies for the picnic. She is going to slice each pie into 8 pieces and serve each person 1 piece. A recipe calls for 1 bag of frozen peaches to make one pie. At the supermarket, Rebekah discovers a sale on frozen fruit. If she buys four bags, she gets the fifth one free. One bag sells for $4.99. How much will it cost Rebekah to buy all the peaches she needs?

$39.92

If Rebekah slices each pie into 10 pieces instead of 8 pieces, how much less will she spend?

$4.99

Ezra went to check out the park where the picnic would be held. He rode his bike to the park 6 miles away from home. He rode to the park at a speed of 12 miles per hour and rode back home at a speed of 18 miles per hour. He left home at 2:30 p.m. and came back at 4:20 p.m. How much time did Ezra spend at the park?

1 hour

Lesson 111

Decimal Place Value & Rounding Decimals

A. Write your answers in the blanks provided.

✓ In 24,539, what is the place value of the digit 2? **Tens**

✓ In 4,112.76, what is the place value of the digit 7? **Tenths**

✓ In 102.358, which digit is in the hundredths place? **5**

✓ In 9.6439, which digit is in the thousandths place? **3**

✓ What number is 100 times larger than 6.14572? **614.572**

B. Round each number to the nearest whole number, tenth, and hundredth.

decimal number	to the nearest whole number	to the nearest tenth	to the nearest hundredth
3.106	3	3.1	3.11
5.273	5	5.3	5.27
4.9358	5	4.9	4.94
3.0529	3	3.1	3.05
139.407	139	139.4	139.41
246.891	247	246.9	246.89

Lesson 112

Decimal Place Value & Multiplication Facts

A. Write each number in standard form.

✓ 5 tens + 2 ones + 8 tenths + 9 thousandths = **52.809**

✓ 7 hundreds + 3 ones + 5 tenths + 1 hundredth = **703.51**

✓ 6 ones + 4 thousands + 8 hundredths + 3 tenths = **4,006.38**

✓ 4 ten thousands + 7 tenths + 2 ones + 9 tens = **40,092.7**

B. Draw lines to match the numbers with their place value descriptions.

21.347	•	• 5 in the hundredths place
13.475	•	• 7 in the thousandths place.
34.758	•	• 8 in the tenths place
47.581	•	• 8 in the hundredths place
75.816	•	• 1 in the tens place

C. Solve the multiplication problems.

27	34	79	95	68
x 93	x 65	x 48	x 25	x 47
2511	2210	3792	2375	3196

Lesson 113

Rounding Decimals & Division Facts

A. Round each number to the nearest whole number, tenth, and hundredth.

decimal number	to the nearest whole number	to the nearest tenth	to the nearest hundredth
1.629	2	1.6	1.63
7.972	8	8	7.97
8.045	8	8	8.05
2.1681	2	2.2	2.17
6.5293	7	6.5	6.53
59.7182	40	39.7	39.72
40.3229	40	40.3	40.32

B. Find the quotient for each division problem.

$$7\overline{)455} = 65 \qquad 4\overline{)356} = 89 \qquad 6\overline{)468} = 78 \qquad 8\overline{)584} = 73$$

Lesson 114

Adding Decimals & Rounding Decimals

A. Add the numbers from left to right and top to bottom to fill in the blanks.

0.7	1.4	2.1
1.6	0.8	2.4
2.3	2.2	4.5

1.5	4.6	6.1
3.9	2.7	6.6
5.4	7.3	12.7

YOUR WORK AREA

2.12	1.94	4.06
0.57	3.36	3.93
2.69	5.3	7.99

B. Round each number to the nearest tenth, hundredth, and thousandth.

decimal number	to the nearest tenth	to the nearest hundredth	To the nearest thousandth
1.5108	1.5	1.51	1.511
3.6379	3.6	3.64	3.638
2.5426	2.5	2.54	2.543
4.7880	4.8	4.79	4.788

Lesson 115

Decimal Number Line

Find the decimal value of each letter marked on the number lines.

A. 1.1 B. 0.3 C. 1.9 D. 1.3 E. 0.2 F. 0.7 G. 1.6 H. 0.6

I. 0.09 J. 0.19 K. 0.04 L. 0.17 M. 0.01 N. 0.08 O. 0.13 P. 0.06

Q. 0.017 R. 0.006 S. 0.012 T. 0.019 V. 0.005 V. 0.003 W. 0.014 X. 0.016

Lesson 116

Telling Time & All Operations

A. Draw the hands on each clock face to show the time.

5:42   8:03   1:19   6:51

B. Complete the equations using +, −, x, and ÷.

3 + 2 = 5	7 − 4 = 3	6 ÷ 2 = 3
7 − 7 = 0	2 x 0 = 0	9 − 4 = 5
9 ÷ 9 = 1	1 + 1 = 2	4 x 2 = 8

C. Solve the problems. Time yourself and find the average time per problem.

34	92	14	23	48	15
+ 58	− 77	x 3	+ 49	− 15	x 5
92	15	42	72	33	75

23	6	14	11	Average time
2)46	9)54	3)42	5)55	

Lesson 117

Elapsed Time & Word Problems

A. Draw the clock hands to show the elapsed time. Write the time beneath.

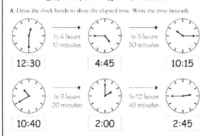

12:30 → In 4 hours 15 minutes → 4:45 → In 5 hours 30 minutes → 10:15

10:40 → In 3 hours 20 minutes → 2:00 → In 12 hours 45 minutes → 2:45

B. Solve each word problem. Use the space on the right for your work area.

Mr. Kim had $868. He bought a TV. Now he has $380 left. How much did the TV cost?

$488

Kate's school has 534 students, and 256 students have pets. How many students have no pets?

278 students

The pet store sold 198 fish today. It has 174 left now. How many fish did the store have at first?

372 fish

Lesson 118

Elapsed Time & Word Problems

A. Find the elapsed time to complete the table.

Start Time	End Time	Elapsed Time
3:00	8:20	5 hours 20 minutes
2:10	10:45	8 hours 35 minute
10:10	3:00	4 hours 50 minute
6:15	3:30	9 hours 15 minute
4:30	8:45	4 hours 15 minute

B. Solve each word problem. Use the space on the right for your work area.

Orson bought 4 movie tickets at $8.75 each. He paid with $50. How much change did he get?

$15

Nancy spent $45.85 on 7 comic books. What was the average cost per book?

$6.55

Mark bought a shirt that cost three times as much as his hat. His hat cost half as much as his gloves. His gloves cost $8.00. How much did Mark spend on his outfit?

$24

Lesson 119

2-D Shapes & Word Problems

A Say the shape names aloud. Cover the names and see if you can remember.

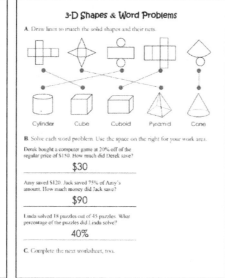

Rectangle Rhombus Trapezoid Parallelogram Pentagon

Hexagon Heptagon Octagon Nonagon Decagon

B Solve each word problem. Use the space on the right for your work area.

Jenny spent 1/6 of her money and saved the rest. What fraction of her money did Jenny save?

5/6

Owen ordered a pepperoni pizza and ate 3/8 of the pizza. What fraction of the pizza was left?

5/8

Emma had 15 cookies. She gave 2/5 of the cookies to Matt. How many cookies were left?

9 cookies

Amy bought 28 apples. She used 1/7 of the apples for cooking. How many apples were left?

24 apples

Lesson 120

3-D Shapes & Word Problems

A Draw lines to match the solid shapes and their nets.

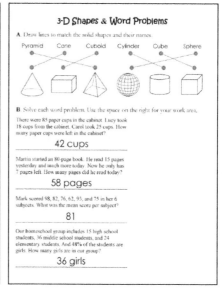

Cylinder Cube Cuboid Pyramid Cone

B Solve each word problem. Use the space on the right for your work area.

Derek bought a computer game at 20% off of the regular price of $150. How much did Derek save?

$30

Amy saved $120. Jack saved 75% of Amy's amount. How much money did Jack save?

$90

Linda solved 18 puzzles out of 45 puzzles. What percentage of the puzzles did Linda solve?

40%

C Complete the next worksheet, too.

Lesson 121

3-D Shapes & Word Problems

A Draw lines to match the solid shapes and their names.

Pyramid Cone Cuboid Cylinder Cube Sphere

B Solve each word problem. Use the space on the right for your work area.

There were 85 paper cups in the cabinet. Lucy took 18 cups from the cabinet. Carol took 25 cups. How many paper cups were left in the cabinet?

42 cups

Martin started an 80-page book. He read 15 pages yesterday and much more today. Now he only has 7 pages left. How many pages did he read today?

58 pages

Mark scored 98, 82, 76, 62, 93, and 75 in her 6 subjects. What was the mean score per subject?

81

Our homeschool group includes 15 high school students, 36 middle school students, and 24 elementary students. And 48% of the students are girls. How many girls are in our group?

36 girls

Lesson 122

3-D Shapes & Counting Coins

A Fill in the properties of 3-D shapes.

Shape	# of Faces	# of Edges	# of Vertices
Cube	6	12	8
Cuboid	6	12	8
Pyramid	5	8	5
Triangular Prism	5	9	6

B Identify which of the above shapes each net makes.

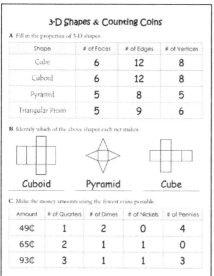

Cuboid Pyramid Cube

C Make the money amounts using the fewest coins possible.

Amount	# of Quarters	# of Dimes	# of Nickels	# of Pennies
49¢	1	2	0	4
65¢	2	1	1	0
93¢	3	1	1	3

Lesson 123

Lines of Symmetry

A Choose True or False for each statement.

A line of symmetry divides a shape into 2 equal parts. **True** False

A circle has infinite (many) lines of symmetry. **True** False

A heart shape has no lines of symmetry. True **False**

A pentagon has more lines of symmetry than a square. **True** False

A square has the same number of lines of symmetry as a rectangle. True **False**

B Draw lines of symmetry on each shape. Write how many there are.

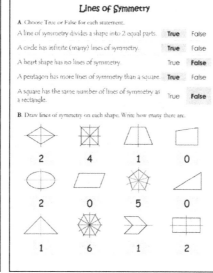

2 4 1 0

2 0 5 0

1 6 1 2

Lesson 124

Types of Angles

A Draw lines to match the angle types with their descriptions.

Acute Angle — Exactly 90°
Right Angle — Less than 90°
Obtuse Angle — Exactly 180°
Straight Angle — Greater than 180° but less than 360°
Reflex Angle — Greater than 90° but less than 180°

B Choose True or False for each statement.

Two parallel lines cross each other. True **False**

Angles around a point always add up to 360°. **True** False

The three angles in a triangle always add up to 180°. **True** False

If we rotate the letter **d** 180° clockwise, it looks like **b**. True **False**

You face north. If you turn 90° clockwise and then 180° counter clockwise, you face west. **True** False

C Classify each angle as acute, right, obtuse, straight, or reflex.

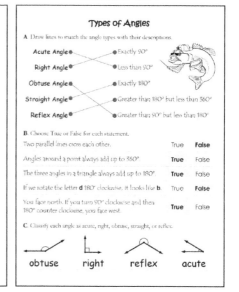

obtuse right reflex acute

Lesson 125

Reading Protractor

Use the protractor to determine each angle formed by two rays.

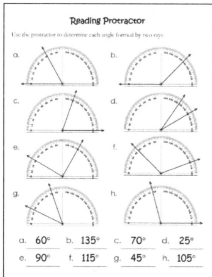

a.
b.
c.
d.
e.
f.
g.
h.

a. **60°** b. **135°** c. **70°** d. **25°**
e. **90°** f. **115°** g. **45°** h. **105°**

Lesson 126

Naming Angles

A Name each angle in two ways using the correct symbols.

∠b = ∠ABC   ∠f = ∠DFE   ∠g = ∠HGI

∠k = ∠JKL   ∠m = ∠OMN   ∠q = ∠VQR

B Classify each angle as acute, right, obtuse, straight, or reflex.

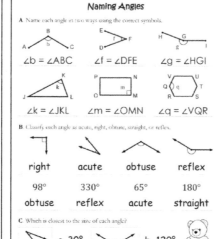

right acute obtuse reflex

98° 330° 65° 180°

obtuse reflex acute straight

C Which is closest to the size of each angle?

a. 30°   b. 120°

Lesson 127

Measurement

A Convert between metric units using the conversion chart below.

1 m = 100 cm   1 km = 1000 m   1 kg = 1000 g   1 L = 1000 ml

30 cm = **0.3** m   0.1 km = **100** m

1.6 kg = **1600** g   700 g = **0.7** kg

2.8 L = **2800** ml   90 ml = **0.09** L

B Solve each word problem. Use the space on the right for your work area.

Derek is 1.36 m tall. His older brother, Jack, is 18 cm taller. How tall is Jack in meters?

1.54 meters

An apple weighs 90 g and the box holds 80 apples. How much does the box weigh in kilograms?

7.2 kilograms

Mary had 1 liter of soda. She drank 300 milliliters. How much soda is left in milliliters?

700 milliliters

A tank held 9.5 liters of water and 650 milliliters was used. How much water is left in liters?

8.85 liters

Lesson 128

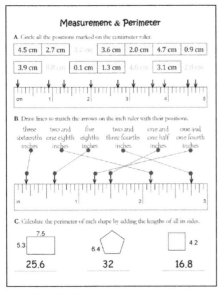

Measurement & Perimeter

A. Circle all the positions marked on the centimeter ruler.

4.5 cm	2.7 cm	3.2 cm	3.6 cm	2.0 cm	4.7 cm	0.9 cm

3.9 cm	0.0 cm	0.1 cm	1.3 cm	4.8 cm	3.1 cm	2.0 cm

B. Draw lines to match the arrows on the inch ruler with their positions.

three sixteenths inches | two and one eighth inches | five eighths inches | two and three fourths inches | one and one half inches | one and one fourth inches

C. Calculate the perimeter of each shape by adding the lengths of all its sides.

25.6   32   16.8

Lesson 129

Perimeter & Area

Find the perimeter (P) and area (A) of each shape.

The area of a rectangle = length (L) x width (W)

14	15 / 4	12 / 5
P = 56	P = 38	P = 34
A = 196	A = 60	A = 60

19 / 17	18 / 36 / 9	40 / 30 / 50 / 20
P = 72	P = 108	P = 220
A = 323	A = 486	A = 1300

YOUR WORK AREA

Lesson 130

Perimeter, Area, & Measurement

A. Find a missing side length on each shape when given the perimeter or area.

Perimeter = 28   Perimeter = 35   Perimeter = 30

a = 7   b = 7   c = 5

Area = 40   Area = 44   Area = 42

d = 8   e = 11   f = 3

B. Convert between units of capacity using the conversion chart below.

1 gallon (gal) = 4 quarts (qt) = 8 pints (pt)
= 16 cups (c) = 128 ounces (oz)

3 gal = 48 c	2 gal = 256 oz
8 qt = 16 pt	12 qt = 48 c
4 pt = 8 c	4 pt = 64 oz
32 c = 256 oz	3 gal = 12 qt

Lesson 131

Addition Practice

Solve the problems. Time yourself on the first three rows. TIME: _____

38	43	42	24	46	39
+ 32	+ 47	+ 9	+ 28	+ 5	+ 29
70	90	51	52	51	68

38	27	43	45	28	34
+ 26	+ 9	+ 36	+ 37	+ 48	+ 5
64	36	79	82	76	39

23	37	32	29	39	50
+ 49	+ 47	+ 5	+ 8	+ 45	+ 26
72	84	37	37	84	76

9565	9354	3795	6519
8199	8697	2546	7673
6847	9075	5609	8752
+ 8054	+ 8412	+ 4686	+ 3254
32,665	35,538	16,636	26,198

Lesson 132

Subtraction Practice

Solve the problems. Time yourself on the first three rows. TIME: _____

42	35	42	45	31	23
- 37	- 9	- 26	- 24	- 2	- 14
5	26	16	21	29	9

37	50	32	43	34	42
- 29	- 39	- 3	- 13	- 26	- 5
8	11	29	30	8	37

21	44	45	27	33	50
- 6	- 20	- 22	- 8	- 17	- 32
15	24	23	19	16	18

8230	6901	7545	9656
- 2065	- 3597	- 4069	- 5768
6165	3304	3476	3888

Lesson 133

Multiplication Practice

Solve the problems. Time yourself on the first three rows. TIME: _____

7	8	6	3	9	4	5	6
x 9	x 4	x 6	x 5	x 5	x 2	x 7	x 8
63	32	36	15	45	8	35	48

8	5	3	0	2	7	9	5
x 8	x 2	x 7	x 2	x 6	x 8	x 4	x 5
64	10	21	0	12	56	36	25

8	3	4	7	5	6	7	6
x 9	x 6	x 9	x 6	x 8	x 1	x 2	x 9
72	18	36	42	40	6	14	54

7778	4060	8751	2575
x 2163	x 3784	x 4214	x 3658
A	B	C	D

A = 16,823,814   C = 36,876,714

B = 15,363,040   D = 9,419,350

Lesson 134

Division Practice

Solve the problems. Time yourself on the first three rows. TIME: _____

7	4	5	1	8
4) 28	5) 20	9) 45	9) 9	3) 24

5	4	10	9	0
6) 30	7) 28	4) 40	6) 54	5) 0

25	9	4	9	8
1) 25	3) 27	9) 36	5) 45	8) 64

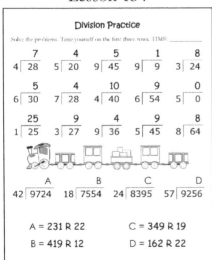

A	B	C	D
42) 9724	18) 7554	24) 8395	57) 9256

A = 231 R 22   C = 349 R 19

B = 419 R 12   D = 162 R 22

Lesson 135

Units of Time & Elapsed Time

A. Convert between units of time using the conversion chart below.

1 day = 24 hours	1 hour = 60 minutes	1 minute = 60 seconds
1 week = 7 days	1 year = 12 months	1 year = 365 days

✓ How many seconds are in 3 minutes? **180 seconds**

✓ How many days are in 8 weeks? **56 days**

✓ How many hours are in 5 days? **120 hours**

✓ How many months are in 4 years? **48 months**

✓ How many minutes are in a quarter of an hour? **15 minutes**

B. Convert between 24-hour time and am/pm notation.

1:24am = **01:24**   2:54pm = **14:54**   23:30 = **11:30pm**

C. Find the time to complete the table.

Start Time	End Time	Elapsed Time
9:00 A.M.	**11:15 A.M.**	2 hours 15 minutes
3:45 P.M.	7:25 P.M.	3 hours 40 minutes
10:15 A.M.	3:55 P.M.	**5 hours 40 minutes**
4:50 A.M.	**2:15 P.M.**	9 hours 25 minutes

Lesson 136

Finding Factors

A. Factors are the numbers that can be divided evenly into a number with no remainder. List all factors of each number.

4	1, 2, 4	12	1, 2, 3, 4, 6, 12
6	1, 2, 3, 6	15	1, 3, 5, 15
8	1, 2, 4, 8	18	1, 2, 3, 6, 9, 18
10	1, 2, 5, 10	20	1, 2, 4, 5, 10, 20

B. Circle the correct answer for each question.

Which number is not a factor of 32? **3** 8 16 32

Which number is not a factor of 24? 1 8 12 **15**

Which number is not a factor of 60? 10 12 **14** 15

Which number is not a factor of 55? 5 11 **25** 55

Which number is a factor of 72? 5 14 **18** 37

Which number is a factor of 80? 15 **20** 30 60

Which number is a factor of 48? **12** 15 20 36

Which number has only one factor? **1** 7 11 37

Lesson 137

Simplifying Fractions

Simplify each fraction as much as possible. Convert your answer to a mixed number if it is an improper fraction.

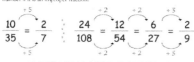

$$\frac{10}{35} = \frac{2}{7} \qquad \frac{24}{108} = \frac{12}{54} = \frac{6}{27} = \frac{2}{9}$$

$$\frac{16}{22} = \frac{8}{11} \qquad \frac{12}{30} = \frac{2}{5} \qquad \frac{18}{12} = \frac{3}{2} = 1\frac{1}{2}$$

$$\frac{40}{72} = \frac{5}{9} \qquad \frac{45}{15} = 3 \qquad \frac{36}{28} = \frac{9}{7} = 1\frac{2}{7}$$

$$\frac{84}{36} = \frac{7}{3} = 2\frac{1}{3}$$

$$\frac{315}{405} = \frac{7}{9}$$

$$\frac{224}{140} = \frac{8}{5} = 1\frac{3}{5}$$

Lesson 138

Adding Fractions

Add the fractions with like denominators. Simplify your answer and convert it to a mixed number, if needed.

$$\frac{5}{7} + \frac{3}{7} = \frac{8}{7} = 1\frac{1}{7} \qquad \frac{2}{18} + \frac{8}{18} = \frac{10}{18} = \frac{5}{9}$$

$$\frac{2}{8} + \frac{9}{8} = \frac{11}{8} = 1\frac{3}{8} \qquad \frac{2}{15} + \frac{3}{15} = \frac{5}{15} = \frac{1}{3}$$

$$\frac{2}{6} + \frac{7}{6} = \frac{9}{6} = 1\frac{1}{2} \qquad \frac{10}{14} + \frac{12}{14} = \frac{22}{14} = 1\frac{4}{7}$$

$$\frac{2}{4} + \frac{5}{4} = \frac{7}{4} = 1\frac{3}{4} \qquad \frac{16}{42} + \frac{19}{42} = \frac{35}{42} = \frac{5}{6}$$

$$7\frac{1}{4} + 2\frac{2}{4} = 9\frac{3}{4} \qquad 9\frac{2}{10} + 2\frac{5}{10} = 11\frac{7}{10}$$

$$3\frac{7}{8} + 2\frac{5}{8} = 6\frac{1}{2} \qquad 5\frac{11}{12} + 3\frac{4}{12} = 9\frac{1}{4}$$

$$5\frac{8}{9} + 3\frac{7}{9} = 9\frac{2}{3} \qquad 2\frac{4}{20} + 4\frac{16}{20} = 7$$

Lesson 139

Subtracting Fractions

A. Subtract the fractions with like denominators. Simplify your answer and convert it to a mixed number, if needed.

$$\frac{2}{8} - \frac{0}{8} = \frac{2}{8} = \frac{1}{4} \qquad \frac{3}{10} - \frac{1}{10} = \frac{2}{10} = \frac{1}{5}$$

$$\frac{4}{9} - \frac{1}{9} = \frac{3}{9} = \frac{1}{3} \qquad \frac{9}{15} - \frac{4}{15} = \frac{5}{15} = \frac{1}{3}$$

$$\frac{7}{6} - \frac{1}{6} = \frac{6}{6} = 1 \qquad \frac{11}{12} - \frac{7}{12} = \frac{4}{12} = \frac{1}{3}$$

$$\frac{5}{4} - \frac{3}{4} = \frac{2}{4} = \frac{1}{2} \qquad \frac{12}{28} - \frac{8}{28} = \frac{4}{28} = \frac{1}{7}$$

$$\frac{1}{2} - \frac{1}{2} = \frac{0}{2} = 0 \qquad \frac{18}{36} - \frac{12}{36} = \frac{6}{36} = \frac{1}{6}$$

B. Can you solve this riddle? Use the clues to find the correct fraction.

$\frac{2}{8}$	$\frac{1}{7}$	$\frac{3}{15}$
$\frac{4}{12}$	$\frac{4}{5}$	$\frac{3}{6}$

I am not equivalent to a third.
I am not in simplest form.
I am less than 0.5.
My denominator is even.
What am I? Circle me!

Lesson 140

Subtracting Fractions

Subtract the fractions with like denominators. Simplify your answer and convert it to a mixed number, if needed.

$$7\frac{3}{4} - 2\frac{1}{4} = 5\frac{1}{2} \qquad 9\frac{7}{10} - 2\frac{2}{10} = 7\frac{1}{2}$$

$$4\frac{3}{5} - 1\frac{2}{5} = 3\frac{1}{5} \qquad 5\frac{11}{12} - 3\frac{3}{12} = 2\frac{2}{3}$$

$$5\frac{8}{9} - 3\frac{5}{9} = 2\frac{1}{3} \qquad 6\frac{16}{20} - 3\frac{1}{20} = 3\frac{3}{4}$$

$$6\frac{5}{6} - 1\frac{1}{6} = 5\frac{2}{3} \qquad 9\frac{19}{25} - 5\frac{14}{25} = 4\frac{1}{5}$$

$$7\frac{1}{4} - 2\frac{3}{4} = 6\frac{5}{4} - 2\frac{3}{4} = 4\frac{2}{4} = 4\frac{1}{2}$$

$$4\frac{1}{8} - 1\frac{5}{8} = 3\frac{9}{8} - 1\frac{5}{8} = 2\frac{4}{8} = 2\frac{1}{2}$$

$$5\frac{4}{9} - 3\frac{7}{9} = 4\frac{13}{9} - 3\frac{7}{9} = 1\frac{6}{9} = 1\frac{2}{3}$$

Lesson 141

Adding Fractions

Add the fractions with like denominators. Simplify your answer and convert it to a mixed number, if needed.

$$\frac{2}{5} + \frac{2}{5} + \frac{4}{5} = \frac{8}{5} = 1\frac{3}{5}$$

$$\frac{6}{8} + \frac{3}{8} + \frac{5}{8} = \frac{14}{8} = \frac{7}{4} = 1\frac{3}{4}$$

$$\frac{3}{9} + \frac{7}{9} + \frac{11}{9} = \frac{21}{9} = \frac{7}{3} = 2\frac{1}{3}$$

$$\frac{5}{10} + \frac{4}{10} + \frac{6}{10} = \frac{15}{10} = \frac{3}{2} = 1\frac{1}{2}$$

$$\frac{7}{12} + \frac{9}{12} + \frac{4}{12} = \frac{20}{12} = \frac{5}{3} = 1\frac{2}{3}$$

$$\frac{6}{15} + \frac{5}{15} + \frac{7}{15} = \frac{18}{15} = \frac{6}{5} = 1\frac{1}{5}$$

$$\frac{9}{21} + \frac{13}{21} + \frac{11}{21} = \frac{33}{21} = \frac{11}{7} = 1\frac{4}{7}$$

$$\frac{15}{36} + \frac{16}{36} + \frac{17}{36} = \frac{48}{36} = \frac{4}{3} = 1\frac{1}{3}$$

Lesson 142

Adding and Subtracting Fractions

Add or subtract the fractions with unlike denominators. To add or subtract fractions with unlike denominators:

First, make the denominators (the bottom numbers) the same.
Second, add or subtract the numerators (the top numbers).
Third, simplify the fraction if needed.

$$\frac{1}{2} + \frac{1}{3} = \frac{1 \times 3}{2 \times 3} + \frac{1 \times 2}{3 \times 2} = \frac{3}{6} + \frac{2}{6} = \frac{5}{6}$$

$$\frac{2}{3} + \frac{1}{4} = \frac{2 \times 4}{3 \times 4} + \frac{1 \times 3}{4 \times 3} = \frac{8}{12} + \frac{3}{12} = \frac{11}{12}$$

$$\frac{2}{9} + \frac{5}{12} = \frac{2 \times 4}{9 \times 4} + \frac{5 \times 3}{12 \times 3} = \frac{8}{36} + \frac{15}{36} = \frac{23}{36}$$

$$\frac{1}{4} - \frac{1}{6} = \frac{1 \times 3}{4 \times 3} - \frac{1 \times 2}{6 \times 2} = \frac{3}{12} - \frac{2}{12} = \frac{1}{12}$$

$$\frac{7}{10} - \frac{9}{15} = \frac{7 \times 3}{10 \times 3} - \frac{9 \times 2}{15 \times 2} = \frac{21}{30} - \frac{18}{30} = \frac{3}{30} = \frac{1}{10}$$

$$\frac{5}{12} - \frac{3}{16} = \frac{5 \times 4}{12 \times 4} - \frac{3 \times 3}{16 \times 3} = \frac{20}{48} - \frac{9}{48} = \frac{11}{48}$$

Lesson 143

Adding Fractions

Add the fractions with unlike denominators. Simplify your answer and convert it to a mixed number, if needed.

$$\frac{2}{3} + \frac{1}{6} = \frac{4}{6} + \frac{1}{6} = \frac{5}{6} \qquad \frac{3}{4} + \frac{1}{3} = \frac{9}{12} + \frac{4}{12} = 1\frac{1}{12}$$

$$\frac{5}{8} + \frac{1}{4} = \frac{5}{8} + \frac{2}{8} = \frac{7}{8} \qquad \frac{7}{8} + \frac{2}{5} = \frac{35}{40} + \frac{16}{40} = 1\frac{11}{40}$$

$$\frac{1}{2} + \frac{1}{6} = \frac{3}{6} + \frac{1}{6} = \frac{2}{3} \qquad \frac{4}{9} + \frac{1}{5} = \frac{20}{45} + \frac{9}{45} = \frac{29}{45}$$

$$\frac{5}{8} + \frac{5}{12} = \frac{15}{24} + \frac{10}{24} = \frac{25}{24} = 1\frac{1}{24}$$

$$\frac{7}{15} + \frac{2}{9} = \frac{21}{45} + \frac{10}{45} = \frac{31}{45}$$

$$\frac{8}{15} + \frac{3}{10} = \frac{16}{30} + \frac{9}{30} = \frac{25}{30} = \frac{5}{6}$$

$$\frac{9}{20} + \frac{5}{12} = \frac{27}{60} + \frac{25}{60} = \frac{52}{60} = \frac{13}{15}$$

Lesson 144

Subtracting Fractions

Subtract the fractions with unlike denominators. Simplify your answer and convert it to a mixed number, if needed.

$$\frac{2}{3} - \frac{1}{6} = \frac{4}{6} - \frac{1}{6} = \frac{1}{2} \qquad \frac{3}{4} - \frac{1}{3} = \frac{9}{12} - \frac{4}{12} = \frac{5}{12}$$

$$\frac{5}{8} - \frac{1}{4} = \frac{5}{8} - \frac{2}{8} = \frac{3}{8} \qquad \frac{7}{8} - \frac{2}{5} = \frac{35}{40} - \frac{16}{40} = \frac{19}{40}$$

$$\frac{1}{2} - \frac{1}{6} = \frac{3}{6} - \frac{1}{6} = \frac{1}{3} \qquad \frac{4}{9} - \frac{1}{5} = \frac{20}{45} - \frac{9}{45} = \frac{11}{45}$$

$$\frac{5}{8} - \frac{5}{12} = \frac{15}{24} - \frac{10}{24} = \frac{5}{24}$$

$$\frac{7}{15} - \frac{2}{9} = \frac{21}{45} - \frac{10}{45} = \frac{11}{45}$$

$$\frac{8}{15} - \frac{3}{10} = \frac{16}{30} - \frac{9}{30} = \frac{7}{30}$$

$$\frac{7}{20} - \frac{1}{12} = \frac{21}{60} - \frac{5}{60} = \frac{16}{60} = \frac{4}{15}$$

Lesson 145

Rounding Numbers

A. Round each number to the nearest ten, hundred, or thousand.

Nearest 10		Nearest 100		Nearest 1000	
8	10	54	100	274	0
47	50	783	800	903	1000
92	90	405	400	2359	2000
235	240	6247	6200	5602	6000

B. Can you solve these riddles? Use the clues to find the correct number.

I am a 2-digit number.
To the nearest 10, I round to 70.
My tens digit is even.
The sum of my digits is 11.
What number am I?

65

I am a 3-digit number.
I am the smallest possible number
that could round to 400 when
rounded to the nearest 100.
What number am I?

350

I am a 2-digit number.
To the nearest 10, I round to 50.
My tens digit is
half of my ones digit.
What number am I?

48

I am a 4-digit number.
I am the largest possible number
that could round to 8000 when
rounded to the nearest 1000.
What number am I?

8499

Lesson 146

Adding Fractions

Add the fractions with unlike denominators. Simplify your answer and convert it to a mixed number, if needed.

$\frac{1}{2} + \frac{2}{6} = \frac{3}{6} + \frac{2}{6} = \frac{5}{6}$

$\frac{3}{5} + \frac{2}{6} = \frac{18}{30} + \frac{10}{30} = \frac{14}{15}$

$\frac{5}{9} + \frac{1}{3} = \frac{5}{9} + \frac{3}{9} = \frac{8}{9}$

$\frac{5}{8} + \frac{1}{3} = \frac{15}{24} + \frac{8}{24} = \frac{23}{24}$

$\frac{7}{8} + \frac{1}{2} = \frac{7}{8} + \frac{4}{8} = 1\frac{3}{8}$

$\frac{4}{6} + \frac{2}{7} = \frac{28}{42} + \frac{12}{42} = \frac{20}{21}$

$\frac{5}{6} + \frac{3}{10} = \frac{25}{30} + \frac{9}{30} = \frac{34}{30} = \frac{17}{15} = 1\frac{2}{15}$

$\frac{9}{14} + \frac{1}{4} = \frac{18}{28} + \frac{7}{28} = \frac{25}{28}$

$\frac{6}{25} + \frac{2}{10} = \frac{12}{50} + \frac{10}{50} = \frac{22}{50} = \frac{11}{25}$

$\frac{9}{20} + \frac{3}{16} = \frac{36}{80} + \frac{15}{80} = \frac{51}{80}$

Lesson 147

Subtracting Fractions

Subtract the fractions with unlike denominators. Simplify your answer and convert it to a mixed number, if needed.

$\frac{1}{2} - \frac{2}{6} = \frac{3}{6} - \frac{2}{6} = \frac{1}{6}$

$\frac{3}{5} - \frac{2}{6} = \frac{18}{30} - \frac{10}{30} = \frac{4}{15}$

$\frac{5}{9} - \frac{1}{3} = \frac{5}{9} - \frac{3}{9} = \frac{2}{9}$

$\frac{5}{8} - \frac{1}{3} = \frac{15}{24} - \frac{8}{24} = \frac{7}{24}$

$\frac{7}{8} - \frac{1}{2} = \frac{7}{8} - \frac{4}{8} = \frac{3}{8}$

$\frac{4}{6} - \frac{2}{7} = \frac{28}{42} - \frac{12}{42} = \frac{8}{21}$

$\frac{5}{6} - \frac{3}{10} = \frac{25}{30} - \frac{9}{30} = \frac{16}{30} = \frac{8}{15}$

$\frac{9}{14} - \frac{2}{5} = \frac{45}{70} - \frac{28}{70} = \frac{17}{70}$

$\frac{6}{25} - \frac{2}{10} = \frac{12}{50} - \frac{10}{50} = \frac{2}{50} = \frac{1}{25}$

$\frac{7}{16} - \frac{3}{20} = \frac{35}{80} - \frac{12}{80} = \frac{23}{80}$

Lesson 148

Multiplying Fractions

Multiply the fractions. Simplify your answer and convert it to a mixed number, if needed.

$\frac{2}{3} \times \frac{3}{8} = \frac{6}{24} = \frac{1}{4}$

$\frac{6}{12} \times \frac{8}{9} = \frac{48}{108} = \frac{4}{9}$

$\frac{3}{4} \times \frac{5}{6} = \frac{15}{24} = \frac{5}{8}$

$\frac{2}{20} \times \frac{5}{6} = \frac{10}{120} = \frac{1}{12}$

$\frac{1}{2} \times \frac{4}{5} = \frac{4}{10} = \frac{2}{5}$

$\frac{3}{18} \times \frac{2}{7} = \frac{6}{126} = \frac{1}{21}$

$\frac{2}{9} \times \frac{3}{8} = \frac{6}{72} = \frac{1}{12}$

$\frac{5}{8} \times \frac{4}{15} = \frac{20}{120} = \frac{1}{6}$

$\frac{5}{6} \times \frac{2}{5} = \frac{10}{30} = \frac{1}{3}$

$\frac{4}{7} \times \frac{14}{16} = \frac{56}{112} = \frac{1}{2}$

$\frac{3}{4} \times \frac{8}{9} = \frac{24}{36} = \frac{2}{3}$

$\frac{5}{9} \times \frac{12}{15} = \frac{60}{135} = \frac{4}{9}$

$\frac{2}{7} \times \frac{3}{4} = \frac{6}{28} = \frac{3}{14}$

$\frac{7}{12} \times \frac{6}{21} = \frac{42}{252} = \frac{1}{6}$

$\frac{2}{9} \times \frac{2}{6} = \frac{4}{54} = \frac{2}{27}$

$\frac{12}{25} \times \frac{10}{16} = \frac{120}{400} = \frac{3}{10}$

Lesson 149

Dividing Fractions

Divide the fractions. Simplify your answer and convert it to a mixed number, if needed.

$\frac{2}{3} \div \frac{1}{3} = \frac{2}{3} \times \frac{3}{1} = \frac{6}{3} = 2$

$\frac{3}{4} \div \frac{5}{8} = \frac{3}{4} \times \frac{8}{5} = \frac{24}{20} = \frac{6}{5} = 1\frac{1}{5}$

$\frac{2}{7} \div \frac{4}{5} = \frac{2}{7} \times \frac{5}{4} = \frac{10}{28} = \frac{5}{14}$

$\frac{8}{9} \div \frac{6}{6} = \frac{8}{9} \times \frac{6}{2} = \frac{48}{18} = \frac{8}{3} = 2\frac{2}{3}$

$\frac{5}{8} \div \frac{5}{14} = \frac{5}{8} \times \frac{14}{5} = \frac{70}{40} = \frac{7}{4} = 1\frac{3}{4}$

$\frac{4}{7} \div \frac{12}{28} = \frac{4}{7} \times \frac{28}{12} = \frac{112}{84} = \frac{4}{3} = 1\frac{1}{3}$

$\frac{7}{12} \div \frac{21}{30} = \frac{7}{12} \times \frac{30}{21} = \frac{210}{252} = \frac{5}{6}$

$\frac{12}{25} \div \frac{16}{45} = \frac{12}{25} \times \frac{45}{16} = \frac{540}{400} = \frac{27}{20} = 1\frac{7}{20}$

Lesson 150

Estimating Sums

Estimate the sums by rounding the numbers to the nearest hundred.

$155 \rightarrow 200$
$+ 108 \rightarrow + 100$
estimate: **300**

$620 \rightarrow 600$
$+ 279 \rightarrow + 300$
estimate: **900**

$974 \rightarrow 1000$
$160 \rightarrow 200$
$+ 223 \rightarrow + 200$
estimate: **1400**

$744 \rightarrow 700$
$200 \rightarrow 200$
$+ 360 \rightarrow + 400$
estimate: **1300**

$870 \rightarrow 900$
$403 \rightarrow 400$
$+ 118 \rightarrow 100$
estimate: **1400**

$659 \rightarrow 700$
$482 \rightarrow 500$
$+ 331 \rightarrow + 300$
estimate: **1500**

$425 \rightarrow 400$
$261 \rightarrow 300$
$918 \rightarrow 900$
$+ 390 \rightarrow + 400$
estimate: **2000**

$385 \rightarrow 400$
$259 \rightarrow 300$
$525 \rightarrow 500$
$+ 108 \rightarrow 100$
estimate: **1300**

Lesson 151

Let's Review! I

A. Complete the problems.

2635	5325	5	8	36	54
+ 4715	− 2647	x 5	x 9	÷ 6	÷ 6
7350	2678	25	72	6	9

B. Count by fourths from 5 to 7.

$5 \quad 5\frac{1}{4} \quad 5\frac{1}{2} \quad 5\frac{3}{4} \quad 6 \quad 6\frac{1}{4} \quad 6\frac{1}{2} \quad 6\frac{3}{4} \quad 7$

C. Solve each word problem. Use the space on the right for your work area.

The store sold 20 cookies for $1.00 each. Their cost per cookie is $0.45. What was the profit?

$11.00

Three children share a box of candies equally. Each gets 7 candies. There are then 2 candies left. How many candies were in the box originally?

23 candies

Find the median and range of Kate's math scores:
92, 84, 81, 76, 93, 76, 85

Median: **84**   Range: **17**

D. Complete the next worksheet, too.

Lesson 151

Let's Review! II

D. Write your answers in the blanks provided.

✓ 700 cm = **7** m   ✓ There are **53** nickels in $2.65.

E. How many obtuse angles are within each shape?

0   **2**   **6**   **1**

F. Find two numbers whose product would be between 250 and 300. Can you find more pairs?

2 x 130 = 260   15 x 18 = 270
3 x 95 = 285   12 x 24 = 288

G. James wants to build a rectangular pen with 16 feet of fencing. Assuming the dimensions (length and width) are to be whole numbers, answer the following.
  a) Draw and label all the possible rectangles that James could make.
  b) Find and record the area of each rectangle.
  c) Color in the rectangle that gives the greatest area.

L = 1	L = 2	L = 3	L = 4
W = 7	W = 6	W = 5	W = 4
A = 7	A = 12	A = 15	A = 16

Lesson 152

Let's Review! I

A. Solve the problems.

57655	71003	100	60	49	32
+ 6847	− 25785	x 3	x 8	÷ 7	÷ 4
64,502	45,218	300	480	7	8

B. Write your answers in the blanks provided.

✓ What is 300 more than 7,845?   **8,145**

✓ What is the product of 3 and 6?   **18**

✓ How many meters are there in 3 kilometers?   **3,000**

✓ It's 2:15 p.m. What time will it be in 45 minutes?   **3:00 pm**

✓ What is the digit in the ten thousands place in 23,954?   **2**

C. Calculate the area (A) of each shape.

A = **60**   A = **56**   A = **82**

D. Complete the next worksheet, too.

Lesson 152

Let's Review! II

D. Solve each word problem. Use the space on the right for your work area.

It takes Laura 15 minutes to walk a mile. How long will it take her to walk 6 miles?

90 minutes

Emily runs 20 miles each week. How many weeks will it take her to run 180 miles?

9 weeks

Sam and Matt have $58 in total. Sam has $10 more than Matt. How much money does Matt have?

$24

Matt is studying 2-D shapes. He drew 3 rectangles and then 2 triangles. If he continues this pattern, what shape will he draw as the 28th shape?

Rectangle

E. Can you solve these riddles? Use the clues to find the correct answer.

I have fewer than 25 coins but more than 10 coins. If I put them in piles of 4 or 5, I have 1 coin left over. How many coins do I have?

21 coins

I have fewer than 40 coins but more than 20 coins. If I put them in piles of 5 or 6, I have 3 coins left over. How many coins do I have?

33 coins

Lesson 153

Let's Review! I

A. Complete the problems.

2485	7005	34	11	20	55
+ 6537	− 4738	+16	x 3	x 7	÷ 5
9,022	2,267	50	33	140	11

B. Write your answers in the blanks provided.

✓ How many 10s are in 10,000? **1,000**

✓ How many nickels are in 4 quarters and 7 dimes? **34**

✓ How many lines of symmetry does a square have? **4**

C. Solve each word problem. Use the space on the right for your work area.

A recipe calls for 2 cups of flour to make 8 servings of a cake. How many cups of flour would you need to make 40 servings of cakes?

10 cups

Mark is making 10 treat bags for his friends. He plans to include a 75¢ orange, a 60¢ apple, and a 25¢ banana. How much money does Mark need?

$16

D. Complete the next worksheet, too.

Lesson 153

Let's Review! II

D. Measure each line to the nearest quarter inch.

1 1/4 inches   **1 3/4** inches   **1 1/2** inches

E. Can you solve these tricky problems? Take your time and think carefully!

1x1, 2x2 squares	4, 1
1x2 or 2x1 rectangles	4
tilted (1 dot enclosed)	1
	10

If you multiply me by 113, subtract 93, divide by 8, and then add 241, you get 300. What number am I? **5**

Leah had a workbook of 300 division problems. On the first day she solved 25 problems. On the second day she solved 12 more problems than the first day. If each day she solved 12 more problems than the day before, on what day would she have completed the workbook?

YOUR WORK AREA **Day 6**

Lesson 154

Let's Review! I

A. Complete the problems.

8329	2400	15	70	30	36
+ 794	− 800	x 4	x 8	÷ 6	÷ 3
9123	1600	60	560	5	12

B. Write your answers in the blanks provided.

✓ How many ounces are in half of a pound? **8 oz**

✓ 5 hundreds + 55 tens + 4 tenths + 24 hundredths = **850.64**

✓ How many pairs of parallel lines does a square have? **2 pairs**

C. Write the fraction that represents the shaded part of each rectangle.

$\frac{1}{4}$ $\frac{1}{6}$ $\frac{3}{8}$

D. Can you solve this geometry puzzle? Take your time and think carefully!

1x1, 2x2, 3x3 squares	9, 4, 1
tilted (1 dot enclosed)	4
tilted (4 dots enclosed)	2
	20

E. Complete the next worksheet, too.

Lesson 154

Let's Review! II

E. Solve each word problem. Use the space on the right for your work area.

Orson bought 4 cookies. He paid $10 and received $0.32 in change. How much did each cookie cost?

$2.42

Monica solved 6 worksheets. Each worksheet had 8 problems. Fifteen of the problems were division. How many problems were not division?

33 problems

Find the median and range of Mia's math scores.
90, 86, 82, 78, 96, 89, 85

Median: **86**   Range: **18**

Mia got 92 and 98 this week. Find the new median and range.

Median: **89**   Range: **20**

How many years would it take you to spend one million dollars if you spend $500 a month?

167 years

How many years would it take you to spend one million dollars if you spend $50 a day?

55 years

Lesson 155

Place Value & Probability

A. Write each number in standard form.

200 + 90 = **290**   7,000 + 100 + 50 = **7,150**

sixty-eight = **68**   eight thousand, three = **8,003**

thirteen thousand, seven hundred twenty-four = **13,724**

B. Write each number in expanded form.

34,035 = **30,000 + 4,000 + 30 + 5**

210,490 = **200,000 + 10,000 + 400 + 90**

C. Write your answers in the blanks provided.

✓ Which fruit will you pick most likely without looking? **apple**

✓ Which fruit will you pick least likely without looking? **banana**

✓ Which is more likely to be picked, a pear or a strawberry? **pear**

✓ What is the percent chance of picking an apple? **40%**

✓ What is the percent chance of picking a strawberry? **20%**

Lesson 156

Addition & Order of Operations

A. Solve the addition problems. Time yourself!   TIME: _____

18	47	34	79	20	64
+ 98	+ 83	+ 20	+ 29	+ 52	+ 75
116	130	54	108	72	139

21	16	46	85	26	78
+ 46	+ 27	+ 63	+ 22	+ 65	+ 87
67	43	109	107	91	165

B. Evaluate each expression using the rules for order of operations.

8 + 4 x 2 = **16**   8 ÷ 2 x 3 − 2 + 6 = **16**

8 x 4 + 2 = **34**   8 ÷ 2 x (3 − 2) + 6 = **10**

8 x (4 + 2) = **48**   8 ÷ 2 x 3 − (2 + 6) = **4**

9 − 3 ÷ 3 = **8**   5 + 3 x (4 + 5) ÷ 3 = **14**

(9 − 3) ÷ 3 = **2**   (5 + 3) x (4 + 5) ÷ 3 = **24**

Lesson 157

Subtraction & Order of Operations

A. Solve the subtraction problems. Time yourself!   TIME: _____

64	52	43	84	77	60
− 17	− 44	− 26	− 65	− 58	− 23
47	8	17	19	19	37

52	33	51	46	65	98
− 25	− 14	− 25	− 38	− 63	− 38
27	19	26	8	2	60

76	61	48	72	50	65
− 40	− 39	− 19	− 46	− 50	− 14
36	22	29	26	0	51

B. Fill in the missing number in each equation.

15 ÷ 3 x 2 = 10   4 x 8 − **5** x 4 = 12

15 − 6 ÷ 3 = 13   2 + 6 ÷ 2 + **5** = 10

6 + **5** x 2 = 16   24 − **8** ÷ 2 x 4 = 8

2 + 3 x **6** = 20   12 ÷ 4 + **9** ÷ 3 = 6

3 x **6** + 6 = 24   20 ÷ 4 x **5** − 5 = 20

Lesson 158

Multiplication & Order of Operations

A. Solve the multiplication problems. Time yourself!   TIME: _____

14	7	5	16	19	8
x 9	x 6	x 8	x 5	x 8	x 6
126	42	40	80	152	48

20	17	9	14	6	18
x 9	x 4	x 9	x 8	x 3	x 7
180	68	81	112	18	126

13	15	6	2	11	2
x 8	x 4	x 9	x 7	x 8	x 5
104	60	54	14	88	10

B. Evaluate each expression using the rules for order of operations.

5 x 8 ÷ 2 + 8 = **28**   5 x 4 ÷ (2 + 8) = **2**

7 + 3 x 2 + 4 = **17**   (7 + 3) x 2 + 4 = **24**

5 x 7 − 5 x 3 = **20**   5 x (7 − 5) x 3 = **30**

9 + 9 ÷ 3 x 6 = **27**   (9 + 9) ÷ 3 x 6 = **36**

16 ÷ 4 x 2 x 5 = **40**   16 ÷ (4 x 2) x 5 = **10**

Lesson 159

Division & Fractions

A. Solve the division problems. Time yourself!   TIME: _____

7) 49 = **7**   4) 60 = **15**   5) 85 = **17**   15) 45 = **3**   14) 70 = **5**

6) 54 = **9**   8) 88 = **11**   4) 68 = **17**   13) 78 = **6**   17) 68 = **4**

B. Add or subtract the fractions with unlike denominators. Simplify your answer and convert it to a mixed number, if needed.

$\frac{8}{9} - \frac{3}{4} = \frac{5}{36}$ $\frac{4}{5} + \frac{2}{3} = \frac{22}{15} = 1\frac{7}{15}$

$\frac{2}{3} - \frac{3}{8} = \frac{7}{24}$ $\frac{1}{2} + \frac{3}{7} = \frac{13}{14}$

$\frac{5}{6} - \frac{2}{7} = \frac{23}{42}$ $\frac{4}{8} + \frac{2}{5} = \frac{36}{40} = \frac{9}{10}$

$\frac{6}{7} - \frac{2}{5} = \frac{16}{35}$ $\frac{4}{5} + \frac{1}{4} = \frac{21}{20} = 1\frac{1}{20}$

Lesson 160

Fractions, Decimals, and Percentages

A. Add, subtract, multiply, or divide the decimals.

$0.8 + 2.5 =$ **3.3** $5.68 \times 10 - 10 =$ **46.8**

$0.25 + 5.9 =$ **6.15** $0.9 \times 50 + 0.2 =$ **45.2**

$40 - 18.7 =$ **21.3** $1.2 \times 0.3 \div 0.4 =$ **0.9**

B. Add, subtract, multiply, or divide the fractions. Simplify your answer and convert it to a mixed number, if needed.

$\dfrac{4}{5} \div \dfrac{2}{7} = \dfrac{14}{5} = 2\dfrac{4}{5}$ $\dfrac{5}{8} \times \dfrac{2}{5} = \dfrac{1}{4}$

$\dfrac{5}{6} - \dfrac{1}{3} = \dfrac{1}{2}$ $\dfrac{6}{7} \times \dfrac{14}{30} = \dfrac{2}{5}$

$\dfrac{1}{2} + \dfrac{2}{5} = \dfrac{9}{10}$ $\dfrac{5}{9} \div \dfrac{25}{54} = \dfrac{6}{5} = 1\dfrac{1}{5}$

C. Calculate the value of each percent.

50% of 18 =   55% of 200 =   YOUR WORK AREA

9   **110**

25% of 40 =   90% of 300 =

10   **270**

Lesson 161

Addition & Coordinate Plane

A. Solve the addition problems.

5588	7132	5607	6273
8754	8275	4482	2348
9767	6359	7365	8564
+ 7651	+ 2630	+ 3887	+ 2397
31,760	**24,396**	**21,341**	**19,582**

B. Write the corresponding letter for each ordered pair.

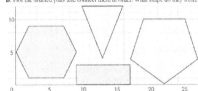

(8,0) **C**   (3,5) **G**

(4,3) **J**   (6,8) **R**

(5,2) **P**   (8,7) **I**

(3,8) **N**   (2,1) **A**

(5,6) **E**   (0,5) **M**

C. Write the corresponding ordered pair for each letter on the above grid.

B **(0, 7)**   D **(6, 4)**   F **(1, 3)**   H **(5, 0)**

K **(7, 2)**   L **(8, 5)**   O **(0, 0)**   Q **(2, 6)**

Lesson 162

Subtraction & Coordinate Plane

A. Solve the subtraction problems.

6504	8352	7437	9020
− 4738	− 5688	− 5869	− 2594
1766	**2664**	**1568**	**6426**

B. Plot the ordered pairs and connect them in order. What shape do they form?

Plot and connect the ordered pairs with lines:	Shape Name
(13, 12) (10, 12) (13, 4) (16, 12) (13, 12)	Triangle
(2, 1) (0, 5) (2, 9) (7, 9) (9, 5) (7, 1) (2, 1)	Hexagon
(9, 0) (13, 0) (17, 0) (17, 3) (13, 3) (9, 3) (9, 0)	Rectangle
(25, 10) (27, 4) (22, 0) (17, 4) (19, 10) (25, 10)	Pentagon

Lesson 163

Multiplication & Coordinate Plane

A. Solve the multiplication problems.

2423	5780	2579	4905
x 8230	x 4163	x 6672	x 2803
A	B	C	D

A = 19,941,290   C = 17,207,088

B = 24,062,140   D = 13,748,715

B. Write the corresponding ordered pair for each letter.

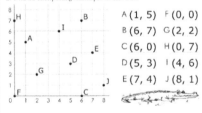

A (1, 5)   F (0, 0)

B (6, 7)   G (2, 2)

C (6, 0)   H (0, 7)

D (5, 3)   I (4, 6)

E (7, 4)   J (8, 1)

Lesson 164

Division & Coordinate Plane

A. Solve the division problems.

	A		B		C		D
22	8085	32	7445	17	5605	32	9843

A = 367 R 11   C = 329 R 12

B = 232 R 21   D = 307 R 19

B. Plot the ordered pairs and connect them in order. What letters do they form?

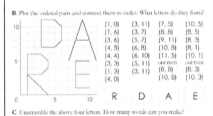

(1, 0)	(3, 11)	(7, 5)	(10, 5)
(1, 6)	(3, 7)	(8, 8)	(8, 5)
(3, 6)	(5, 7)	(9, 11)	(8, 3)
(4, 5)	(6, 8)	(10, 8)	(8, 1)
(4, 4)	(6, 10)	(11, 5)	(10, 1)
(3, 3)	(5, 11)	LINE ENDS	LINE ENDS
(1, 3)	(3, 11)	(8, 8)	(8, 3)
(4, 0)		(10, 8)	(10, 3)

R   D   A   E

C. Unscramble the above four letters. How many words can you make?

DARE, READ, DEAR

Lesson 165

Coordinate Plane & Reading Numbers

A. Write the corresponding letter for each ordered pair.

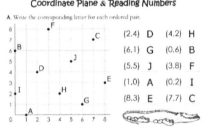

(2,4) **D**   (4,2) **H**

(6,1) **G**   (0,6) **B**

(5,5) **J**   (3,8) **F**

(1,0) **A**   (0,2) **I**

(8,3) **E**   (7,7) **C**

B. Write each number in words. The first one is done for you.

387	three hundred eighty-seven
625	six hundred twenty-five
849	eight hundred forty-nine
792	seven hundred ninety-two
461	four hundred sixty-one
204	two hundred four
530	five hundred thirty

Lesson 166

Probability

A. Choose True or False for each statement.

Probability is how likely something is to happen.   **True**   False

A high probability means an event is unlikely to occur.   True   **False**

Probabilities can be expressed as fractions, decimals, or percentages.   **True**   False

B. Choose the correct probability of each event.

The probability of an event that will never occur is   **0**   0.5   1

The probability of an event that will definitely occur is   0   0.5   **1**

The probability of rolling a 3 with a die is   **1/6**   1/3   1/2

The probability of getting a head on a coin toss is   0   0.2   **0.5**

The probability of rolling an odd number with a die is   0   10%   **50%**

C. A bag contains 12 marbles. Four of them are red and the rest are blue. Find the probability of each event. A probability of an event occurring is

$$\text{A probability of an event occurring} = \frac{\text{The number of favorable outcomes}}{\text{The number of possible outcomes}}$$

The probability of pulling out a red marble =   **1/3**

The probability of pulling out a yellow marble =   **0**

The probability of pulling out a red or blue marble =   **1**

Lesson 167

Probability

A. Write the probability of each event as a fraction. Simplify your answer.

The probability of 7 favorable outcomes and 28 possible outcomes =   **1/4**

The probability of 4 favorable outcomes and 36 possible outcomes =   **1/9**

The probability of 9 favorable outcomes and 72 possible outcomes =   **1/8**

B. The spinner is spun. Find the probability of each event as a fraction.

The probability of landing on 1 =   **1/4**

The probability of landing on 8 =   **0**

The probability of not landing on 3 =   **5/8**

The probability of landing on 2 or 4 =   **3/8**

C. A die is rolled. Find the probability of each event as a fraction.

The probability of rolling a 5 or smaller =   **5/6**

The probability of rolling greater than a 4 =   **1/3**

The probability of rolling a multiple of 3 =   **1/3**

The probability of rolling a multiple of 5 =   **1/6**

The probability of rolling factors of 30 =   **5/6**

The probability of rolling factors of 50 =   **1/2**

Lesson 168

Probability

A. Find the probability of each event as a percent.

The probability of an event that is certain to occur =   **100%**

The probability of an event that is impossible to occur =   **0%**

The probability of an event that evenly may or may not occur =   **50%**

B. A number is chosen at random from 1 to 50. Find the probability of each event as a fraction. Simplify your answer.

The probability of choosing an odd number =   **1/2**

The probability of choosing a number greater than 30 =   **2/5**

The probability of choosing a number with 2 in tens place =   **1/5**

C. A month is chosen at random from a year. Find the probability of each event as a fraction. Simplify your answer.

The probability of choosing February =   **1/12**

The probability of choosing a month ending with R =   **1/3**

The probability of choosing a month starting with J =   **1/4**

The probability of choosing an even numbered month =   **1/2**

YOUR WORK AREA

Lesson 169

Possible Outcomes

Find the number of possible outcomes for each problem.

For a weekend trip, Ron packed 3 shirts (red, blue, and green) and 2 pairs of pants (black and blue). How many different outfits can Ron make?

6 outfits

The café sells fruit smoothies. You can choose a small, medium, or large smoothie. You can choose bananas, kiwis, or oranges. How many choices of smoothies are offered by the café?

9 choices

Jenny wanted a sandwich for lunch. In the kitchen, she found ham, tuna, turkey, and roast beef. She also found white, wheat, and rye bread. How many different sandwiches can Jenny make?

12 sandwiches

Sam, Eric, Zoe, and Eli like to play tennis with one another. How many singles matches are possible among the four friends?

6 matches

Note that there are 6 duplicate combinations.

Brian is walking to the park. He wants to stop by the library on the way. From his house, there are 2 routes to the library. From the library, there are 4 routes to the park. How many different routes are there from Brian's house to the park?

8 routes

Lesson 170

Making Predictions

A. Choose True or False for each statement.

A prediction is a guess about what will happen.
True False

A prediction is always right.
True **False**

The more possible outcomes there are, the harder it is to make an accurate prediction.
True False

B. Solve each word problem. Use the space on the right for your work area.

Kyle predicts that if a letter is chosen randomly from the 26 letters in the alphabet, the probability of choosing a vowel is equal to that of choosing a consonant. Is his prediction correct?

No, it's not correct.

Laura predicts that if a number is chosen randomly from 1 to 100, the probability of choosing a number with 5 in tens place is equal to that of choosing 5 in ones place. Is her prediction correct?

Yes, it's correct.

If you roll a dice 300 times, approximately how many times would you predict rolling a 6?

50 times

Mason predicted that he would score an average of at least 85 on his math quizzes this month. Here are his scores.
78, 96, 89, 85, 80, 90, 86, 84

Yes, it was correct.

Lesson 171

Units of Measurement

A. Choose True or False for each statement.

Two major systems of measurement in use today are the customary system and the metric system.
True False

The customary system is used in the United States while the metric system is used in most countries.
True False

The customary system is used in math and science.
True **False**

Inch, pound, gallon, and Fahrenheit are metric units.
True **False**

B. Choose the best customary and metric units for each measurement.

Pounds	Meters	Ounces	Gallons
Liters	Fahrenheit	Grams	Miles
Kilograms	Feet	Celsius	Kilometers

I want to measure...	customary unit	metric unit
The distance between two cities	Miles	Kilometers
The weight of a baby elephant	Pounds	Kilograms
The amount of water in a tub	Gallons	Liters
Today's temperature	Fahrenheit	Celsius
The height of a pine tree	Feet	Meters
The weight of one cookie	Ounces	Grams

Lesson 172

Units of Length

A. Choose the most appropriate customary unit for each measurement.

| Inches | Feet | Yards | Miles |

The height of a man	**feet**	The width of a book	**inches**
The length of a fence	**yards**	The height of a house	**feet**
The length of a pencil	**inches**	The perimeter of a lot	**yards**
The distance between two planets in our solar system			**miles**

B. Convert between units of length using the conversion chart below.

1 feet (ft) = 12 inches (in)   1 mile (mi) = 5,280 feet (ft)
1 yard (yd) = 3 feet (ft)   1 mile (mi) = 1,760 yards (yd)

5 ft = **60** in   7,040 yd = **4** mi

9 yd = **27** ft   15,840 ft = **3** mi

6 mi = **10,560** yd   63,360 in = **1** mi

YOUR WORK AREA

Lesson 173

Measurement Tools

A. Choose the most appropriate tool for each measurement.

| Scale | Stopwatch | Measuring Cup | Beaker |
| Ruler | Tape measure | Protractor | Thermometer |

I want to measure...	I'd use...
Today's temperature	Thermometer
The angle of a triangle	Protractor
The perimeter of a watermelon	Tape measure
The height of a math workbook	Ruler
The weight of a basket of apples	Scale
The amount of milk to bake cookies	Measuring Cup
The amount of liquid in a science class	Beaker
The time in seconds to run a 100-meter race	Stopwatch

B. Draw lines to match the measurement tools with the units they measure in.

Scale   Thermometer   Ruler   Protractor   Beaker

Centimeters   Milliliters   Grams   Celsius   Degrees

Lesson 174

Measuring Length

Get your ruler. Use the line segments below to complete the worksheet.

a. ━━━   b. ━━   c. ━━
d. ━━━   e. ━━
f. ━━━━

A. Measure each line segment to the nearest half centimeter.

a. **5** cm   b. **3** cm   c. **4.5** cm
d. **5.5** cm   e. **9** cm   f. **13.5** cm

B. Measure each line segment to the nearest inch.

a. **2** in   b. **1** in   c. **2** in
d. **2** in   e. **4** in   f. **5** in

C. Measure each line segment to the nearest quarter inch.

a. **2** in   b. **1 1/4** in   c. **1 3/4** in
d. **2 1/4** in   e. **3 1/2** in   f. **5 1/4** in

D. Can you solve this riddle?

Temperature

Lesson 175

Finding Volume

A. Count the unit cubes to find the volume (V) of each shape.

The volume of a shape = the number of unit cubes needed to fill it

V = **12** cubic units   V = **18** cubic units   V = **30** cubic units

B. Find the volume (V) of each rectangular prism (or cuboid).

The volume of a rectangular prism = length (L) x width (W) x height (H)

V = **168**   V = **264**   V = **420**

C. Find the volume (V) of each cube.

The volume of a cube = length (S) x width (S) x height (S) = S³

V = **125**   V = **343**   V = **729**

Lesson 176

Telling Temperature

A. Read the temperature shown on each thermometer.

43 °F   **78** °F   **119** °F   **45** °C   **72** °C   **97** °C

B. Convert between Fahrenheit and Celsius using the conversion chart below.

Formula to convert °C to °F   Formula to convert °F to °C
(C x 9) / 5 + 32 = F   (F - 32) x 5 / 9 = C

Human body temperature   Rabbit's body temperature
37°C = **98.6** °F   101°F = **38.3** °C

YOUR WORK AREA

Lesson 177

Telling Time

A. Choose True or False for each statement.

The short hand on a clock tells you the minute.
True **False**

There are 5 minutes between each number on a clock.
True False

A quarter hour is equal to 30 minutes and a half hour is equal to 15 minutes.
True **False**

B. Write the time beneath each clock.

3:42   **7:03**   **2:19**   **11:41**

C. Write each time in digital form.

eight o'clock **8:00**   half past seven **7:30**

quarter to four **3:45**   quarter past twelve **12:15**

The short hand is between 1 and 2. The long hand is on 8.   **1:40**

The short hand is between 9 and 10. The long hand is on 5.   **9:25**

Lesson 178

Units of Time

A. Complete the conversion chart for time units.

1 day =	**24** hours	1 week =	**7** days
1 hour =	**60** minutes	1 year =	**12** months
1 minute =	**60** seconds	1 year =	**365** days

B. Convert between units of time using the conversion chart above.

- How many seconds are in 9 minutes? **540**
- How many hours are 2400 minutes? **40**
- How many hours are in 7 days? **168**
- How many weeks are 224 days? **32**
- How many days are in 4 years? **1,460**
- How many seconds are in half a day? **43,200**

YOUR WORK AREA

Lesson 179

Elapsed Time

Solve each word problem. Use the space on the right for your work area.

The baseball game started at 9:15 a.m. and ended at noon. How long was the game?

2 hours 45 minutes

Kyle watched a movie for 2 hours and 15 minutes. He started at 11:45 a.m. When did he finish it?

2:00 p.m.

The class starts at 9:10 a.m. If it starts in 25 minutes, what time is it now?

8:45 a.m.

The holiday sale started at 11 a.m. Monday and lasted for 24 hours. When did it end?

11 a.m. Tuesday

The festival began at 9 a.m. Friday and ended at 5 p.m. Sunday. How long was the festival?

2 days 8 hours

The train departed at 3 p.m. Tuesday and arrived at 8 a.m. Wednesday. How long did it take?

0 days 17 hours

A summer camp started at 1 p.m. Monday and lasted 7 days and 4 hours. When did it end?

5 p.m. the next Monday

Lesson 180

Mystery Numbers

Find the mystery numbers. Can you follow the steps mentally?

4 x 1000 = 4000
50% of 4000 = 2000 → **2000**

75 / 5 + (3 x 60) = 195 → **195**

27 / 100 = 0.27
The nearest tenth of 0.27 = 0.3 → **0.3**

(50 + (2 x 24)) x 2 = 196
The nearest ten of 196 = 200 → **200**

The nearest 1000 of 3141.59 = 3000
3000 / 6 = 500 → **500**

24 / 4 x 100 − 3 = 597 → **597**

We hope you had a great year with EP Math 4.

EP provides free, complete, high quality online homeschool curriculum for children around the world. Find more of our courses and resources on our site, allinonehomeschool.com.

If you prefer offline materials, consider Genesis Curriculum which takes a book of the Bible and turns it into daily lessons in science, social studies, and language arts for your children to learn all together. The curriculum also includes learning Biblical languages. Genesis Curriculum offers Rainbow Readers and a new math curriculum, A Mind for Math, which is also done all together and is based on each day's Bible reading. GC Steps is an offline preschool and kindergarten program. Learn more about our expanding curriculum on our site, genesiscurriculum.com.

Made in the USA
Las Vegas, NV
15 September 2021